JOURNEY TO ALLAH SERIES

ADHERING TO THE STRAIGHT PATH
Amidst Confusion

FAITH Publications

All thanks are due to Allah *subhaanahu wa ta'ala* for enabling us with this effort. Special thanks to the following contributors:

Content Writer: Sheikh Sulejman Dzanic
Editing Team: Amber Bokhari, Safi Khan, Abdul Qaadir Abdul Khaaliq
Curriculum Coordinator: Samira Hingoro
Graphic and Layout Design: Farah Firman
Published by FAITH Publications

Copyright © 2025 FAITH Publications
2nd Edition

All rights reserved. No part of this publication may be reproduced, distributed, or transmitted in any form or by any means, including photocopying, recording, or other electronic or mechanical methods, without the prior written permission of the publisher, except in the case of brief quotations embodied in critical reviews and certain other noncommercial uses permitted by copyright law. *Printed in the United States of America*.

ISBN 979-8-9897920-7-8

For permission requests, write to the publisher at the address below.

FAITH Publications
5301 Edgewood Road
College Park, MD 20740, USA
Phone: 301-982-9848
email: info@faithpublications.org
www.faithpublications.org

TABLE OF CONTENTS

UNIT 1 | ISLAM & DEVIATION

CHAPTER	PG	
01	11	WHICH PATH SHOULD I TAKE?
02	19	ERRANT BELIEFS AMONG THE MUSLIMS
03	41	IS THIS REALLY ISLAM?

UNIT 2 | COMMON DEVIATIONS

CHAPTER	PG	
04	57	INTRODUCTION
05	61	JUDAISM & CHRISTIANITY
06	73	HINDUISM & BUDDHISM
07	81	DEISM, AGNOSTICISM, & ATHEISM

PREFACE

In today's ever-changing world, a common cry you hear among Muslims when forced to make a decision in life is, "I am so confused!" With the rise of social media, it has led everyone to have an opinion, regardless of whether it's right or wrong or whether it's based on a personal viewpoint or evidence-based. Sometimes, with multiple views and ways within Islam of handling complex decisions, people feel lost. How does one navigate which path leads and guides to decisions that will ensure Allah's Happiness? *Adhering to the Straight Path Amidst Confusion* aims to highlight the path trodden by the Prophet *sallAllahu 'alayhi wa salaam* and his Companions *radhiAllahu 'anhum*. This book briefly discusses some of the common sects within Islam as well as some of the prevalent ideologies outside Islam.

Our belief system has been meticulously preserved for over fourteen centuries, and our faith has always proved its truth when challenged by every man-made ideology or interpretation. A proper understanding of our faith will anchor us in today's world of doubts, disbelief, and self-centeredness. This book will help us begin our journey to know and understand some of the prevalent ideologies in society so that we can identify them and protect ourselves from them. The main goal in learning is not to label each other but so that we do not fall into these beliefs that may go against the *Qur'an* and *Sunnah* (the middle path) or take us out of the fold of Islam. Thus, distancing us from Allah in this life and the next.

Adhering to the Straight Path Amidst Confusion is part of a new, courageous Islamic Studies curriculum. Specially developed to help us apply our faith to real-world issues. Features like the *Did You Know?* boxes and the *Review and Reflect* sections show everyday, practical applications of our belief. In addition, all the *hadith* references cited in this book are authentic. We pray that this curriculum helps us draw closer to Allah. We would love to improve this curriculum with your suggestions. Please send your feedback to info@faithpublications.org. Lastly, we would like to thank Sh. Sulejman Dzanic for writing this book beautifully. May Allah accept the effort of everyone who worked on this curriculum, and more importantly, may Allah accept our efforts to get closer to Him.

UNIT 1
ISLAM & DEVIATION

UNIT 1
IMPORTANT VOCABULARY

'ADL
Divine Justice

AHLUL-BAYT
A title referring to the family of the Prophet sallAllahu 'alayhi wa sallam.

AHLUS-SUNNAH WAL-JAMA'AH
Belief of those who take their belief from the *Qur'an* and the *Sunnah* as practiced by the Prophet sallAllahu 'alayhi wa sallam, his Companions radhiAllahu 'anhum, the first three generations of Muslims, and the pious predecessors.

AR-RUBOOBIYYAH
The Lordship

'AQEEDAH
Islamic belief

'AQL
Intellect

DHIKR
Remembrance of Allah

HIJRAH
Migration

IJMAA'
Consensus

IMAN
Faith

JAMA'AH
Group

KHALIFAH
Caliph; leader of the Muslims.

KHAWARIJ
The first sect that appeared in Islam.

KUFR
Disbelief

MURJI'AH
Emerged as a theological school opposed to the *Khawarij*.

MU'TAZILAH
A sect that emerged in the second century of the *hijrah*.

NAFS
Self; soul

QADR
Divine decree

QUR'ANIYOON
Emerged as a sect within Islam that prioritizes the *Qur'an* as the exclusive source of guidance.

SHAYTAAN
Devil

SHI'A
Amongst the first sects that appeared splitting from *Sunni* Islam.

SUNNAH
It is the way of the Prophet Muhammad *sallAllahu 'alayhi wa sallam*, his life, his teachings, his words (orders and prohibitions), his tacit approvals, actions, character, and physical traits.

SUNNI
Person who follows the *Sunnah* (way of the Prophet *sallAllahu 'Alayhi wa sallam*). This is the practice of the majority of the Muslims.

TABI'EEN
The generation of Muslims who came after the Companions of the Prophet *sallAllahu 'alayhi wa sallam*.

TAWHEED
The Oneness of Allah

TAZKIYATUN-NAFS
Purification of the soul

UMMAH
Muslim community

WASAT
Middle

WASATIYYAH
The middle path; a concept of maintaining a balanced approach between being excessive and deficient in all aspects of life.

TABLE OF CONTENTS

UNIT 1 | ISLAM & DEVIATION

CHAPTER	PG	
01	11	WHICH PATH SHOULD I TAKE?
02	19	ERRANT BELIEFS AMONG THE MUSLIMS
03	41	IS THIS REALLY ISLAM?

ESSENTIAL QUESTIONS

This unit is designed to help answer the following questions.

1. Why is it important to take the middle path in Islam?
2. How does Islam view extremism?
3. Why is it important to know about prevalent ideologies in society?
4. How can one identify deviations in Islamic belief?
5. How does deviation in belief impact one's Hereafter?

CHAPTER 1

WHICH PATH SHOULD I TAKE?

Islam was revealed by Allah as a comprehensive way of life. Allah has filled the *Qur'an* with many lessons that we may learn from and apply in our lives in order to gain His pleasure. Sometimes, in life, we face situations where people go to extremes, ignoring the middle path. For example, most people in the world today focus on the needs of the body alone (i.e., its pleasures, likes, dislikes, etc.). They believe that success only comes through material progress. On the other hand, there are many who focus only on the spirituality of the heart (i.e., being a recluse, monk, nun, etc.). This group believes that success can only be measured spiritually by divorcing yourself from the worldly life completely. In contrast to these two views, Islam takes the middle path. Success in Islam is achieved by engaging both the body and the soul in a balanced way. Hence, Islam emphasizes participation in the material world to advance spiritually. Therefore, for a Muslim to enrich his or her faith, he or she must care about his or her fellow human beings.

THE MIDDLE PATH

The concept of how to maintain a balanced approach in our lives is a guiding principle in Islam. This is the concept of the middle path, also known as **"wasatiyyah"** in Arabic.

The middle path means **staying away from extremes or excesses in our beliefs and actions while also making sure that we are not careless or negligent about those same beliefs and actions.**

The concept of the middle path can be understood from the following *ayah*. Allah tells us,

وَكَذَٰلِكَ جَعَلْنَٰكُمْ أُمَّةً وَسَطًا لِّتَكُونُوا۟ شُهَدَآءَ عَلَى ٱلنَّاسِ وَيَكُونَ ٱلرَّسُولُ عَلَيْكُمْ شَهِيدًا

"And thus We have made you a community justly balanced, that you will be witnesses over the people and the Messenger will be a witness over you...." [1,2]

In another *ayah* Allah says,

اهْدِنَا ٱلصِّرَٰطَ ٱلْمُسْتَقِيمَ

"Guide us to the straight path." [3]

In the above *ayah*, Allah describes the middle path as a "straight path," emphasizing it is the path of guidance, truth, and justice. It is the first path that is blessed by Allah. This is the path that the Prophet *sallAllahu 'alayhi wa sallam* and his Companions *radhiAllahu 'anhum* were upon. This is considered the *Sunni* Muslim belief. It is also called the belief of **Ahlus-Sunnah wal-Jama'ah**. This means the belief of those who take their belief from the *Qur'an* and the *Sunnah* as practiced by the Prophet *sallAllahu 'alayhi wa sallam*, his Companions *radhiAllahu 'anhum*, the first three generations of Muslims, and the pious predecessors who came after them. [4]

---

1. Surah Al-Baqarah [2:143]
2. Imam At-Tabari *rahimahullaah* said regarding this *ayah*, "My view is that Allah described them as "*wasat*" due to their moderation in religion. They are not extremists in it, like the Christians who went to extremes and attributed things to 'Isa *'alayhis salaam* that he did not say. Nor are they people of negligence in it, like the negligence of the Jews who altered the book of Allah..." *(Tafseer At-Tabari)*
3. Surah Al-Fatihah [1:6]
4. Pious people of the past.

صِرَٰطَ ٱلَّذِينَ أَنْعَمْتَ عَلَيْهِمْ غَيْرِ ٱلْمَغْضُوبِ عَلَيْهِمْ وَلَا ٱلضَّآلِّينَ

"The path of those upon whom You have bestowed favor, not of those who have evoked [Your] anger or of those who are astray." 5

In the previous *ayah* Allah is describing three paths. The first path is the path which is blessed by Allah. This is the path of those who have knowledge and practice it. The second path is that which evokes Allah's anger. This is the path of those who have the correct knowledge but do not practice it. The third path is the path of those who have gone astray. This is the path of those who practice without the correct knowledge.

The Prophet *sallAllahu 'alayhi wa sallam* told us,

فَإِنَّهُ مَنْ يَعِشْ مِنْكُمْ فَسَيَرَى اخْتِلَافًا كَثِيرًا فَعَلَيْكُمْ بِسُنَّتِي وَسُنَّةِ الْخُلَفَاءِ الرَّاشِدِينَ الْمَهْدِيِّينَ عَضُّوا عَلَيْهَا بِالنَّوَاجِذِ، وَإِيَّاكُمْ وَمُحْدَثَاتِ الْأُمُورِ؛ فَإِنَّ كُلَّ بِدْعَةٍ ضَلَالَةٌ

"He among you who lives long enough will see many differences. So for you is to observe my Sunnah and the Sunnah of the rightly-principled and rightly-guided successors, holding on to them with your molar teeth. Beware of newly-introduced matters, for every innovation 6 (bid'ah) is an error." 7

DEVIATION FROM THE MIDDLE PATH

Have you ever thought about why people stray from the middle path? Since the beginning of Islam, some individuals and groups have gone from this middle path and strayed in matters of '**Aqeedah** (Islamic belief). People stray from the middle path when they use their rationale and intellect instead of Revelation. Especially when people misinterpret or use their own interpretations of things that are unseen or beyond human comprehension and reach extreme and faulty beliefs. Such things are only known through Revelation. This is how different ideologies and sects emerged within the Muslims. The Prophet *sallAllahu 'alayhi wa sallam*, foretold this when he said,

"My ummah will divide into 73 sects; all of them will be in the Fire except for one, and that is the Jama'ah." 8 It was said, *"And who are they, O Allah's Messenger?"* He *sallAllahu 'alayhi wa sallam* responded, *"That which I and my Companions are upon today."* 9

This *hadith* teaches us that the *ummah* will divide into many groups and sects and that there is only one true path, and all other paths are deviations. This understanding can also

---

5 Surah Al-Fatihah [1:6-7]
6 Innovation here means innovation in Islamic belief and practices and not in scientific advancements.
7 At-Tirmidhi and Abu Dawood
8 Group
9 At-Tirmidhi and Abu Dawood

be seen in the following *hadith*. 'Abdullah ibn Mas'ud [10] *radhiAllahu 'anhu* narrated that, "Allah's messenger *sallAllahu 'alayhi wa sallam* *drew a line for them and then said, "This is God's path." Thereafter he drew several lines on his right and left and said, "These are paths, on each of which there is a devil who invites people to follow it." And he recited, "And that this is my path, straight; follow it…"* [11]

This *hadith* provides additional clarification on the concept of the middle path, emphasizing that it represents the straight path of Allah without any deviation. It signifies that any other paths or ideologies are deviations that lead away from the true path of Allah.

EARLY SECTS AND IDEOLOGIES

Studying early sects and ideologies is necessary to gain a better understanding of what the middle path is. Only when we understand and recognize extremism can we steer clear of it. Following the Prophet *sallAllahu 'alayhi wa sallam* and his Companions *radhiAllahu*

---

10 Famous companion who was best known for his interpretation of the *Qur'an* and narrations of *hadith*. (d.650AD)
11 Ahmad

'anhum will help us adopt a balanced approach in our beliefs and a balanced way of life that will solicit the pleasure of Allah.

Let us briefly examine two examples from early sects. One such sect within Islam is known as the **Khawarij**. This group took their beliefs to extreme measures, claiming that Muslims who commit major sins lack true *iman* (faith) and consequently are not Muslims. This deviation from the *Sunni* belief led to division and war within the Muslims. Another sect, the **Murji'ah**, [12] held the view that acts of worship and deeds are unrelated to one's *iman*. These two groups adopted opposing extremes: one excessively emphasizing major sins as grounds for expulsion from Islam, while the other group was exceedingly lenient, granting sinners the assurance that their actions would not affect their status as faithful believers. However, **the balanced approach lies between these two extremes.** Muslims who commit major sins are still considered Muslims, but they are urged to refrain from sinning and should seek repentance from Allah. Furthermore, actions are an integral part of *iman*, and Muslims should actively engage in righteous deeds while maintaining hope in Allah's mercy and reward.

---

12 This sect appeared as a result of the controversy around the deaths of the 3rd and 4th *Khalifah*; 'Uthman and 'Ali *radhiAllahu 'anhum*. Emerged as a theological school that was opposed to the *Khawarij* on questions related to early controversies regarding sin and definitions of what is a true Muslim. Their belief is opposite to the belief of *Khawarij*. They went to the opposite extremes by taking disobedience and sins lightly. Where they believe in the hope of Allah's Mercy to the extent that Allah will forgive one regardless of their lack of practice of Islam.

WHO ARE THE **BEST PEOPLE** TO ALIGN **OUR BELIEFS** WITH?

When faced with different sects and ideologies, each claiming to be on the "straight path," it becomes crucial to determine which group or ideology is truly on the right path. The Prophet *sallAllahu 'alayhi wa sallam* taught us a method to identify such sects or ideologies. He *sallAllahu 'alayhi wa sallam* told us to follow,

"That which I and my Companions are upon today." [13]

In another *hadith*, the Prophet *sallAllahu 'alayhi wa sallam* specified the first three generations of Islam as being the best. He *sallAllahu 'alayhi wa sallam* tells us,

"The best people are those of my generation, and then those who will come after them (the next generation), and then those who will come after them (i.e., the next generation)." [14]

Hence, our belief should align with the belief as practiced by the Prophet *sallAllahu 'alayhi wa sallam*, his Companions *radhiAllahu 'anhum* and the first three generations of Muslims. [15]

By examining these sects or ideologies, we can look at their fundamental beliefs and teachings. Are they aligned with the teachings and practices of the Prophet *sallAllahu 'alayhi wa sallam* and his Companions? If they deviate from this standard, it signifies that they are not on the right path and belong to a stray group that does not adhere to the path of the Prophet *sallAllahu 'alayhi wa sallam* and his Companions *radhiAllahu 'anhum*.

---

13   At-Tirmidhi

14   Al-Bukhari

15   The first generation of Muslims is the generation of the Prophet *sallAllahu 'alayhi wa sallam* and his Companions *radhiAllahu 'anhum*; the second generation of Muslims which came after the Companions of the Prophet *sallAllahu 'alayhi wa sallam* are known as the *Tabi'un*; third generation of Muslim who came after the Tabi'un are known as *Tabi' Tabi'un*. They are also referred to as the pious predecessors.

In Islam, adhering to the middle path is very important because it teaches us to avoid extremism and negligence in our beliefs and practices. By adhering to this path, we can avoid falling into misguided sects and following deviant ideologies. In the next chapters, we will explore various sects and ideologies, learning how they deviated from the middle path and strayed from the true teachings of Islam. By learning about these sects and ideologies, we can have a better understanding of the consequences of straying from the middle path. This will help us appreciate the middle path and remain steadfast upon seeking the pleasure of Allah.

CHAPTER 2

ERRANT BELIEFS AMONG THE MUSLIMS

During the 1400 years of Islamic history, several sects have emerged with beliefs not practiced by the Prophet *sallAllahu 'alayhi wa salaam* and the early Muslims. In this chapter, we will explore a few prominent sects that have developed within Islam. We will examine a brief background and history of each group in order to have a better understanding of the driving forces behind their emergence. We will also learn about their core beliefs and practices and how they strayed from the true teachings of Islam. It is important to note that even though the beliefs and practices of some of these sects can be considered **kufr** (disbelief), our aim is to better understand how these sects strayed from the true path of Islam in order to foster better dialogue and understanding.

THE MAIN GROUPS IN ISLAM

Islam has two major groups. Every sect is within these two groups. If they don't fall within these groups, then their beliefs have been altered so much that they are not considered Muslims anymore. The two major groups in Islam are:

1. SUNNI

This is mainstream Islam, which believes in and practices Islam the way the Prophet *sallAllahu 'Alayhi wa sallam* and his Companions *radhiAllahu 'anhum* did. Approximately 85-90% of Muslims today practice *Sunni* Islam.

2. SHI'A

This division started after the death of the Prophet *sallAllahu 'Alayhi wa sallam* who believed that his son-in-law, 'Ali ibn Abi Talib *radhiAllahu 'anhu* should have been given the leadership of the Muslims after his death. We will discuss this sect more in detail later in this book. Approximately 10-15% percent of Muslims follow this sect. Some of the sects under the *Shi'a* have extreme beliefs that take them outside the fold of Islam.

Following are some of the prominent sects within *Sunni* Islam.

THE KHAWARIJ

The **Khawarij** are considered the first sect to appear in *Sunni* Islam. The name *Khawarij* comes from the Arabic word "*kha-ra-ja*," which means went out or seceded. They are known by this name because they went out against 'Ali ibn Abi Talib [16] *radhiAllahu 'anhu* and seceded from his army. They are also known as **Haruriyah**, from Harura, a village close to Kufa, Iraq.

BACKGROUND

The *Khawarij* first emerged during the time of the fourth **Khalifah (Caliph)**, [17] 'Ali ibn Abi Talib *radhiAllahu 'anhu*. During his time as *khalifah*, there was a power struggle between him and Muawiyyah ibn Abi Sufyan [18] *radhiAllahu 'anhu*, who was the governor of *Sham*. [19] This political unrest in the *ummah* eventually led to the Battle of *Siffin*. [20] The battle lasted for months, and many Muslim lives were lost. Some of the companions of the Prophet *sallAllahu 'alayhi wa sallam* suggested arbitration [21] in order to settle things and avoid further bloodshed. Initially, all parties agreed except a group from 'Ali ibn Abi Talib *radhiAllahu 'anhu's* side, who broke away because of their belief that arbitration is disbelief. They held the view that only Allah has the right to judge between people, and to bring someone in as an arbitrator was negating this belief. 'Ali ibn Abi Talib, 'Abdullah ibn 'Abbas, and other companions *radhiAllahu 'anhum* refuted this belief, quoting an *ayah* from the *Qur'an* where Allah says,

وَإِنْ خِفْتُمْ شِقَاقَ بَيْنِهِمَا فَٱبْعَثُوا۟ حَكَمًا مِّنْ أَهْلِهِ وَحَكَمًا مِّنْ أَهْلِهَا إِن يُرِيدَآ إِصْلَـٰحًا يُوَفِّقِ ٱللَّهُ بَيْنَهُمَآ إِنَّ ٱللَّهَ كَانَ عَلِيمًا خَبِيرًا

"If you anticipate a split between them, appoint a mediator from his family and another from hers. If they desire reconciliation, Allah will restore harmony between them. Surely Allah is All-Knowing, All-Aware." [22]

---

16 The cousin and son-in-law of the Prophet *sallAllahu 'alayhi wa sallam* who was the 4th Rightly-Guided *Khalifah*. (d.661AD)

17 Caliph is the leader or ruler of the Muslims; A successor to the Prophet *sallAllahu 'alayhi wa sallam*.

18 Famous companion of the Prophet *sallAllahu 'alayhi wa sallam*, one of the scribes of revelation, and the 6th *Khalifah* of the Muslims.

19 Greater Syria; Sham was commonly used during the rule of the Muslim *Khalifahs* to describe the area between the Mediterranean and the Euphrates, Anatolia (in present day Turkey) and Egypt.

20 The Battle of Siffin was fought in 657CE.

21 A process of resolving disputes between parties using a neutral third party.

22 Surah An-Nisaa' [4:35]

This understanding meant that Allah not only permits arbitration, but also commands it, as in the case of divorce. This response was strong enough to have some of the *Khawarij* return to the correct path, but many others remained astray. The *Khawarij* were then quickly defeated and scattered throughout the *ummah*. Over the course of our history, they have emerged many times and are even present in our time today.

EXTREMISM IN BELIEF

The *Khawarij* hold very distinct beliefs because of their literal and extreme interpretation of the *Qur'an* and *Sunnah*. Among their core beliefs are:

- *Iman* does not increase or decrease, and if a Muslim leaves any obligatory act, they are devoid of *iman*.
- Committing major sins removes one from the fold of Islam.
- They believe it is permissible to use violence against unjust rulers and fellow Muslims who disagree with them.

These extreme beliefs and others exemplified their shallow understanding of the *Qur'an* and *Sunnah*, which caused them to deviate from *Sunni* Islam.

An example of their superficial understanding of the *Qur'an* is when the *Khawarij* ultimately withdrew from the army of 'Ali ibn Abi Talib *radhiAllahu 'anhu* because they misunderstood the *ayah*,

إِنِ ٱلْحُكْمُ إِلَّا لِلَّهِ

"The decision is only for Allah." [23]

According to their understanding, 'Ali *radhiAllahu 'anhu* committed disbelief for agreeing to arbitration, which is the judgment of men and not Allah. However, 'Abdullah ibn 'Abbas [24] *radhiAllahu 'anhu* who was known among the Companions of the Prophet *sallAllahu 'alayhi wa sallam* for his understanding of the *Qur'an*, refuted them with the *Qur'an*, quoting the *ayah*:

يَٰٓأَيُّهَا ٱلَّذِينَ ءَامَنُوا۟ لَا تَقْتُلُوا۟ ٱلصَّيْدَ وَأَنتُمْ حُرُمٌۭ وَمَن قَتَلَهُۥ مِنكُم مُّتَعَمِّدًۭا فَجَزَآءٌۭ مِّثْلُ مَا قَتَلَ مِنَ ٱلنَّعَمِ يَحْكُمُ بِهِۦ ذَوَا عَدْلٍۢ مِّنكُمْ

"O you who have believed, do not kill game [25] *while you are in the state of ihram. And whoever of you kills it intentionally - the penalty is an equivalent from sacrificial animals to what he killed, as judged by two just men among you..."* [26]

---

23 Surah Al-'An'aam [6:57]
24 One of the cousins of the Prophet *sallAllahu 'alayhi wa sallam* who was best known for his expertise in the interpretation of the *Qur'an*. (d.687AD)
25 Game in this *ayah* refers to any animal that is hunted for food or other.
26 Surah Al-Ma'idah [5:95]

The Khawarij were refuted from the same Qur'an they recite because they lacked the proper understanding; they went astray from the straight path, as the Prophet sallAllahu 'alayhi wa sallam said about them,

"People who would recite the Qur'an with their tongues and it would not go beyond their collar bones..." [27]

THE DEVIATION OF THE KHAWARIJ

The Prophet sallAllahu 'alayhi wa sallam cautioned us about the Khawarij and their misguidance. He sallAllahu 'alayhi wa sallam said,

"There will arise at the end of time a people young in age and weak in intellect. Their speech will be that of the best of creation. They will recite the Qur'an but it will not go beyond their throats. They will shoot through the religion just like an arrow goes through the game..." [28]

The extreme path taken by the Khawarij should teach us several things:

- The Qur'an and Sunnah need to be understood in a comprehensive manner because a shallow understanding can lead to deviation from the true path.

- We learn that the Qur'an and Sunnah need to be understood in their proper context as they were revealed to the Prophet sallAllahu 'alayhi wa sallam, and as practiced by his Companions radhiAllahu 'anhum.

- The importance of seeking the proper understanding of Islam to prevent such misguidance and fanaticism as the Khawarij.

---

27 Sahih Muslim
28 Sahih Al-Bukhari

SUMMARY: THE KHAWARIJ

- The first sect which appeared among the Sunni Muslims.

- It emerged during the time of the fourth Khalifah 'Ali ibn Abi Talib radhiAllahu 'anhu.

Among their core beliefs...

They believe that iman does not increase or decrease.

They believe it is permissible to fight Muslims who disagree with them.

They believe that failing to do something obligatory or committing a major sin constitutes disbelief.

DID YOU KNOW?

Allah tells us,

قُلْ يَٰعِبَادِىَ ٱلَّذِينَ أَسْرَفُوا عَلَىٰٓ أَنفُسِهِمْ لَا تَقْنَطُوا مِن رَّحْمَةِ ٱللَّهِ ۚ إِنَّ ٱللَّهَ يَغْفِرُ ٱلذُّنُوبَ جَمِيعًا ۚ إِنَّهُۥ هُوَ ٱلْغَفُورُ ٱلرَّحِيمُ

Say, "O My servants who have transgressed against themselves [by sinning], do not despair of the mercy of Allah. **Indeed, Allah forgives all sins**. *Indeed, it is He who is the Forgiving, the Merciful."* [29]

---

[29] Az-Zumar [39:53]

THE MU'TAZILAH

The **Mu'tazilah** are a sect among the Sunni Muslims that emerged in the second century of the **hijrah (migration)**. [30] The name "Mu'tazilah" comes from the Arabic word "*i'tazala*", which means "to withdraw." This name was given to the group because they diverged from the clear teachings of Islam. According to certain accounts, their name originates from the act of one of their scholars, Wasil ibn Ata, [31] who distanced himself from the teachings of Hasan Al-Basri [32] *rahimahullaah*, marking the beginning of this sect. This sect first originated in Basra, present-day Iraq, and has throughout history spread through the *Muslim community*.

BACKGROUND

The emergence of the *Mu'tazilah* sect can be attributed to the introduction of new ideas into the Muslim community, particularly stemming from the translation of Greek philosophy into Arabic. Some of these ideas were the belief in ultimate free will, which led to the rejection of **qadr** (divine decree) and negation of certain Names and Attributes of Allah that appeared to contradict reason and logic. These various developments, alongside other contributing factors, led to the rise of the distinct *Mu'tazilah* sect.

BELIEFS OF THE MU'TAZILAH

The *Mu'tazilah* sect holds several distinctive beliefs in '*Aqeedah* that diverge from the correct understanding of the *Qur'an* and *Sunnah*. Firstly, they emphasize **tawheed** (the Oneness of Allah) in a misguided way. They believe Allah is unique in such an extreme way that He does not really have any attributes. They fear that this would make His attributes similar to human beings. They also believe in **'adl** (divine justice) in a deviant way. They claim that Allah's actions are governed by rational principles as understood by their intellect. He would never act unjustly according to their perception of justice. Hence, they deny that everything (including the actions of His creation) is the creation of Allah. Therefore, according to them, human actions are not created or influenced by Allah and are instead created by humans. This belief led them to reject the concept of **qadr** (the divine decree) in favor of advocating free will for humans unaffected by the **qadr** (according to their perception).

Another belief is their assertion that the *Qur'an* was created and not the literal word of Allah. They rationalize this by arguing that if the *Qur'an* was uncreated and the speech of Allah, it would compromise

---

30   The *Hijrah* is when the Prophet *sallAllahu 'alayhi wa sallam* migrated with his Companions *radhiAllahu 'anhum* from Makkah to Madinah in 622 CE in order to escape persecution. When explaining timelines of events in Islamic history, it is common to refer to the years before or after the *hijrah*.
31   Lived in Basra and introduced the *Mu'tazilah* belief. Born in the Arabian Peninsula in 700 CE.
32   Famous Scholar from the 2nd generation of Muslims *(Tabi'een)* (642-728 CE).

the concept of *tawheed*, suggesting that Allah's speech is not eternal; rather, it is changeable. Additionally, the *Mu'tazilah* placed a strong emphasis on ***aql*** (intellect) and reasoning to interpret Islamic teachings. They give precedence to their own intellectual deductions, even when they contradict certain actions or attributes of Allah confirmed by the *Qur'an*, leading them to negate many of Allah's Names and Attributes based on their rational conclusions.

WHY BELIEVING IN QADR (DIVINE DECREE) IS IMPORTANT?

As discussed earlier, the *Mu'tazilah* sect rejects the concept of *Qadr*. Let us explore what *Qadr* is and why believing in it is important. It is important to believe in *Qadr*, as it is one of the pillars of *Iman*, and negating it takes you outside the fold of Islam. *Qadr* means that Allah has already decreed our destiny, and we believe that all good and bad of divine decree comes from Allah. However, we do not know our destiny. We have been given free choice to make decisions in our life. Allah, in His Knowledge, knows what decisions we will take since He knows the future. It is important to know that Allah has already ordained our *qadr*. Knowing and believing in *qadr* also helps us not to complain or regret lost opportunities or various life decisions or actions.

The Prophet *sallAllahu 'alayhi wa sallam* told us,

"... If anything befalls you, do not say, "If only I had done such and such" rather say "**Qaddar-Allahu wa ma sha'a fa'al** (Allah has decreed and whatever He wills, He does)." For (saying) "If" opens (the door) to the deeds of *Shaytaan*." [33]

While our *qadr* has been decreed for us, Allah can change our *qadr* by our sincere *du'aas*. Allah, in His Mercy, gives us several opportunities to be better human beings. His Love and Mercy for us are shown in His being able to change our *qadr* when we make sincere *du'aas*.

---

33   Ibn Majah

DEVIATION OF THE MU'TAZILAH

The main reason the *Mu'tazilah* went astray is because they gave precedence to reason and intellect over revelation, the *Qur'an*, and authentic *Sunnah*. In contrast, the belief of *Ahlus-Sunnah wal-Jama'ah* is that it gives precedence to authentic revelation over one's own reasoning. A guiding principle is that a sound mind will not contradict authentic revelation because the mind is created by Allah and the revelation comes from Allah, so there cannot be any contradiction between revelation and the reasoning and intellect Allah created; both are from Allah.

As believers, the proper attitude is to submit and accept whatever Allah and His Messenger *sallAllahu 'alayhi wa sallam* have decreed, even if we do not know the wisdom behind it. Allah explicitly tells us,

وَمَا كَانَ لِمُؤْمِنٍ وَلَا مُؤْمِنَةٍ إِذَا قَضَى ٱللَّهُ وَرَسُولُهُ أَمْرًا أَن يَكُونَ لَهُمُ ٱلْخِيَرَةُ مِنْ أَمْرِهِمْ ۗ وَمَن يَعْصِ ٱللَّهَ وَرَسُولَهُ فَقَدْ ضَلَّ ضَلَٰلًا مُّبِينًا

"It is not for a believing man or a believing woman, when Allah and His Messenger have decided a matter, that they should [thereafter] have any choice about their affair. And whoever disobeys Allah and His Messenger has certainly strayed into clear error." [34]

---

34   Surah Al-Ahzaab [33:36]

Opposing the command of Allah is akin to following the path of **Shaytaan**. When Allah created Adam *'alayhis salaam*, He instructed Iblees [35] to prostrate before him, but he disobeyed Allah due to his own reasoning. Iblees rationalized his refusal, claiming that he, being made of fire, was superior to Adam *'alayhis salaam*, who was created from clay.

Allah says,

قَالَ مَا مَنَعَكَ أَلَّا تَسْجُدَ إِذْ أَمَرْتُكَ ۖ قَالَ أَنَا خَيْرٌ مِّنْهُ خَلَقْتَنِى مِن نَّارٍ وَخَلَقْتَهُ مِن طِينٍ

"What prevented you from prostrating when I commanded you?" [Satan] said, "I am better than him. You created me from fire and created him from clay." [36]

The main lesson we learn is the importance of adhering to revelation and putting it above our own intellect and reasoning. The *Mu'tazilah* went astray when they prioritized human reasoning and intellect over divine revelation. In contrast, the belief of *Ahlus-Sunnah wal-Jama'ah* is to rely on and follow the guidance provided by Allah in the *Qur'an* and the teachings of the Prophet *sallAllahu 'alayhi wa sallam*. This lesson highlights the significance of grounding our beliefs and actions in the authentic sources of Islam and not relying solely on human intellect or rationalizations.

---

35   Iblees is the name used to refer to **Shaytaan** (Satan), and also the leader of the *shayateen* (devils)
36   Surah Al-A'raaf [7:12]

SUMMARY: THE MU'TAZILAH

- Appeared in the second century of the hijrah.

- Emerged due to introducing new ideas into the Muslim community, stemming from the translation of Greek philosophy into Arabic.

Among their core beliefs...

They give precedence to rationale and Intellect over Revelation. (They place emphasis on the intellect and reasoning to interpret Islamic teachings, even when they contradict the Qur'an.)

They reject the concept of qadr in favor of advocating free will.

They believe the Qur'an was created, and not the speech of Allah.

> ### DID YOU KNOW?
>
> 'Ali ibn Abi Talib *radhiAllahu 'anhu* said, "If the religion were based upon one's opinion, one might expect the bottom of the leather sock to be wiped instead of the top. I have seen the Messenger of Allah, *sallAllahu 'alayhi wa sallam*, wiping over the upper part of his leather socks." [37]

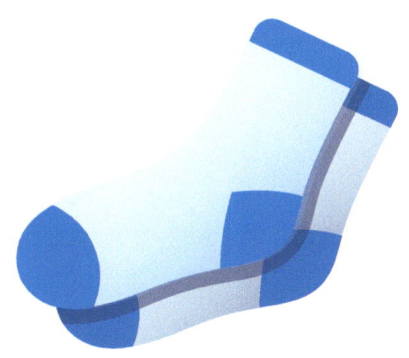

THE QUR'ANIYOON

The **Qur'aniyoon**, also referred to as Qur'anists or Qur'an-only Muslims, are a sect within Islam that prioritizes the *Qur'an* as the exclusive source of guidance while rejecting the authority of the *hadith* and *Sunnah*. The roots of the *Qur'aniyoon* can be traced back to the early centuries of Islam, when discussions regarding the sources of jurisprudence took place. The movement recently experienced significant growth, largely in response to contemporary challenges and debates surrounding the authenticity and interpretation of the *hadith* and *Sunnah* of Prophet Muhammad *sallAllahu 'alayhi wa sallam*.

HISTORY OF THE QUR'ANIYOON

As mentioned earlier, the *Qur'aniyoon* sect can be traced back to early Islamic history. However, the organization of the movement occurred much later, gaining momentum in the 20th century. Individuals like Rashad Khalifa, an Egyptian-American, played a significant role in advocating for sole adherence to the *Qur'an* while rejecting the *hadith*. Khalifa's assertion that he discovered a mathematical code within the *Qur'an* further popularized the concept of a self-sufficient *Qur'an*-centric approach. It is worth noting that later, Rashad Khalifa claimed prophethood himself, ironically becoming the interpreter of the *Qur'an*. Despite such controversies, the *Qur'aniyoon* movement has slowly gained followers globally, attracting individuals who may not have a comprehensive understanding of Islam and the sciences of the *hadith*. [38]

---

37   Abu Dawood
38   Refers to the study of *hadith* (Its classification, types, preservation and methodology of grading *hadith*, etc.).

BELIEFS OF THE QUR'ANIYOON

The *Qur'aniyoon* hold that the *Qur'an* is the complete and final revelation from Allah and is sufficient as the sole source of guidance for Muslims. They argue that the *hadith* and *Sunnah* are susceptible to human error and distortion over time. As a result, they reject the authenticity and reliability of the *hadith* and *Sunnah*, viewing it as a later development not sanctioned by the *Qur'an* itself. The *Qur'aniyoon* prioritize a direct and individual literal interpretation of the *Qur'an*, relying on the verses alone to formulate their beliefs and practices.

The Importance of Sunnah

It is agreed by scholars throughout Islamic history that Islamic laws are derived from the *Qur'an* and *Sunnah* of the Prophet Muhammad *sallAllahu 'alayhi wa sallam* and then the consensus of the scholars of the Muslim Ummah. The *Sunnah* provides clarification of the laws mentioned in the *Qur'an*. It is also considered Revelation from Allah in the words of the Prophet *sallAllahu 'alayhi wa sallam* as

Qur'an & Sunnah

Allah informs us in the *Qur'an*,

وَمَا يَنطِقُ عَنِ ٱلْهَوَىٰٓ إِنْ هُوَ إِلَّا وَحْىٌ يُوحَىٰ

"Nor does he (the Prohpet sallAllahu 'alayhi wa sallam) speak from (his own) inclination. It is not but a revelation revealed." [39]

Following the path of the *Qur'aniyoon* would mean going against Allah's command, as Allah has explicitly instructed believers to obey the Prophet's *sallAllahu 'alayhi wa sallam* guidance with the same importance as obeying Allah Himself. Allah tells us,

مَّن يُطِعِ ٱلرَّسُولَ فَقَدْ أَطَاعَ ٱللَّهَ وَمَن تَوَلَّىٰ فَمَآ أَرْسَلْنَـٰكَ عَلَيْهِمْ حَفِيظًا

*"He who obeys the Messenger has obeyed Allah ; but those **who turn away - We have not sent you over them as a guardian.**"* [40]

---

39 Surah An-Najm [53:3-4]
40 Surah An-Nisaa' [4:80]

The *Qur'aniyoon* sect refers to themselves as believers, but the *Qur'an* defines true belief as wholeheartedly accepting the Prophet's sallAllahu 'alayhi wa sallam judgments without discomfort or dispute. Allah says,

فَلَا وَرَبِّكَ لَا يُؤْمِنُونَ حَتَّىٰ يُحَكِّمُوكَ فِيمَا شَجَرَ بَيْنَهُمْ ثُمَّ لَا يَجِدُوا فِي أَنفُسِهِمْ حَرَجًا مِّمَّا قَضَيْتَ وَيُسَلِّمُوا تَسْلِيمًا

"But no, by your Lord, they will not [truly] believe until they make you, [O Muhammad], judge concerning that over which they dispute among themselves and then find within themselves no discomfort from what you have judged and submit in [full, willing] submission." [41]

These *ayaat* and others serve as clear proof of the misguidance of the *Qur'aniyoon* sect and their deviation from true guidance. Rejecting the *Sunnah* and *hadith* of the Prophet sallAllahu 'alayhi wa sallam leads a person to reject the *Qur'an* which ultimately leads one to *kufr*.

The Prophet sallAllahu 'alayhi wa sallam himself predicted about the *Qur'aniyoon*. He warned that a time would come when people would reject his *Sunnah* and *hadith*, relying solely on the *Qur'an* for determining what is lawful and unlawful.

As he sallAllahu 'alayhi wa sallam told us, *"Lo! Soon a hadith from me will be conveyed to a man, while he is reclining on his couch, and he says: 'Between us and you is Allah's Book. So whatever we find in it that is lawful, we consider lawful, and whatever we find in it that is unlawful, we consider it unlawful.' Indeed whatever the Messenger of Allah sallAllahu 'alayhi wa sallam made unlawful, it is the same as what Allah made unlawful."* [42]

In terms of the authenticity of the *hadith* and Sunnah, those who have studied hadith and its sciences know and understand that it has been meticulously preserved, compiled, and authenticated. To reject the *hadith* and *Sunnah* on the basis of believing that they are susceptible to human error and distortion over time is a belief based on ignorance and human opinion instead of facts.

---

41   Surah An-Nisaa' [4:65]
42   At-Tirmidhi

SUMMARY: THE QUR'ANIYOON

- Appeared in early Islamic history when discussions arose around the authority of the Qur'an and the hadith.

- It emerged as a sect within Islam that prioritizes the Qur'an as the exclusive source of guidance while rejecting the authority of the hadith and Sunnah.

Among their core beliefs...

They believe that the Qur'an is the complete and final revelation from Allah and is sufficient as the sole source of guidance for Muslims.

They reject the hadith and Sunnah as they believe they are susceptible to human error and distortion over time.

They take literal interpretations of the Qur'an, relying on the verses alone to formulate their beliefs and practices.

DID YOU KNOW?

The Prophet sallAllahu 'alayhi wa sallam said, "Let me not find one of you reclining on his couch, when a command or prohibition of mine comes to him, and he says: 'I do not know, we only follow what we find in the Book of Allah.'" [43]

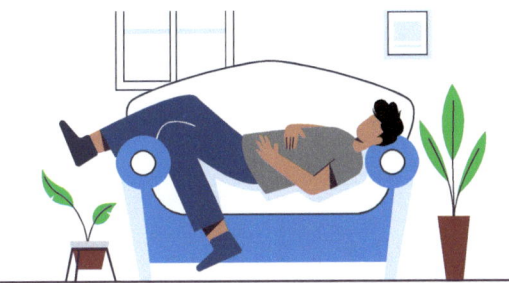

THE SHI'A

The *Shi'a* as mentioned earlier, are one of the major sects of Islam. It is also considered one of the first sects to emerge in Islam. The term "**Shi'a**" is an Arabic word meaning "supporter" or "group," which is in reference to "*Shi'atu 'Ali*," which is "the party of 'Ali." The *Shi'a* believe that 'Ali ibn Abi Talib radhiAllahu 'anhu, the cousin of Prophet Muhammad sallAllahu 'alayhi wa sallam, was the rightful successor to the Prophet sallAllahu 'alayhi wa sallam as the leader of the Muslim community.

BACKGROUND

The *Shi'a* sect emerged as a split from *Sunni* Islam because of a disagreement over the leadership after the death of Prophet Muhammad sallAllahu 'alayhi wa sallam. The *Shi'a* believe that 'Ali ibn Abi Talib radhiAllahu 'anhu, should have been the first successor of Prophet Muhammad sallAllahu 'alayhi wa sallam while **Sunnis** believe in the righteous *Khalifahs*: Abu Bakr, 'Umar, 'Uthman, and then 'Ali radhiAllahu 'anhum.

Throughout history, the *Shi'a* sect split even further into several major sects that differed from each other in terms of their beliefs and practices. These include the Twelver *Shi'a* sect, which is also known as "*Ithna Ash'ari*." They are the majority of *Shi'a* worldwide. Other sects include the Zaidi, 'Alawi, and Ismaili *Shi'a*. There are certain extreme beliefs within these sects that can take one outside the fold of Islam. Some of these extreme beliefs include identifying certain attributes of Allah with His creation and claiming prophethood after the last and final messenger. [44] For example, the *'Alawi* sect is considered to be outside the fold of Islam due to their belief in considering 'Ali radhiAllahu 'anhu as divine and a reincarnation of God on Earth. This belief is totally away from mainstream Islam.

---

43 At-Tirmidhi
44 Reference: Contemporary Sects Affiliated with Islam and Clarification of Islam's Stance Toward Them.

SHI'A BELIEFS

Despite the many sects within the *Shi'a* understanding of Islam, there are common beliefs that they all share. One of the central beliefs is their concept of **Imamate**, which holds that *Imams* are divinely appointed and are responsible for the spiritual and political status of the Muslim community. *Shi'as* believe that their *Imams* are infallible and that they receive special guidance and knowledge from Allah. The *Shi'as* also believe that the *Imams* are descended from the family of the Prophet sallAllahu 'alayhi wa sallam, that is why they have extreme love and reverence for the family of the Prophet sallAllahu 'alayhi wa sallam which includes 'Ali, Fatimah, and their sons Hasan and Husayn radhiAllahu 'anhum. They also emphasize the concept of commemorating the martyrdom of Husayn [45] radhiAllahu 'anhu, the grandson of the Prophet sallAllahu 'alayhi wa sallam.

EXTREMISM IN LOVE

As Muslims, it is an integral part of our faith to love and show the utmost respect for the Prophet sallAllahu 'alayhi wa sallam, his family (referred to as *Ahlul-Bayt*), and his Companions radhiAllahu 'anhum. However, it is important to make sure that this love does not lead us away from the true teachings of Islam. The Prophet sallAllahu 'alayhi wa sallam himself emphasized the importance of loving his family and his Companions.

WHO ARE THE AHLUL-BAYT?

The term *Ahlul-Bayt* refers to the family of the Prophet Muhammad sallAllahu 'alayhi wa sallam. According to our scholars, it includes his wives, his descendants, the descendants of Banu Hashim, Banu Muttalib, and their freed slaves, as well as the families of 'Ali, 'Abbas, Ja'far, 'Aqil, and Al-Harith ibn 'Abd Al-Muttalib radhiAllahu 'anhum.

---

45 The martyrdom of Husayn *radhiAllahu 'anhu*, the grandson of the Prophet *sallAllahu 'alayhi wa sallam* at Karbala (city in present day Iraq) was a historical tragedy. Many *Shi'a* go to extremes to commemorate this tragic day (10th of Muharram) by beating their chests, slapping their cheeks, etc. All these acts go against the teachings of Islam. The Prophet *sallAllahu 'alayhi wa sallam* said, *"He is not one of us who strikes his cheeks, rends his garment, or cries with the cry of the Jahiliyyah (Days of Ignorance)."* (Sahih Al-Bukhari and Sahih Muslim).

The Prophet *sallAllahu 'alayhi wa sallam* said, "Love Allah for what He nourishes you with of His Blessings, love me due to the love of Allah, and love the people of my house due to love of me." [46]

The Prophet *sallAllahu 'alayhi wa sallam* also forbade cursing his Companions *radhiAllahu 'anhum*, showing their importance and significance in Islam. He *sallAllahu 'alayhi wa sallam* said,

"Do not revile my Companions, do not revile my Companions. By Him in Whose Hand is my life, if one amongst you would have spent as much gold as Uhud, it would not amount to as much as one much on behalf of one of them or half of it." [47]

Many followers of the *Shi'a* sect have gone to extremes in their love for the Prophet *sallAllahu 'alayhi wa sallam's* family, especially for 'Ali, Fatimah *radhiAllahu 'anhum*, and their descendants, who are revered as the *Imams* of the *Shi'a*. This extremism has led them to attribute infallibility [48] to the *Imams* and some even believe that they receive divine revelations and knowledge from Allah. Such views, however, contradict the teachings of the *Qur'an* and *Sunnah*, leading many to deviate from the true path of Islam.

Islam teaches love and respect towards the Prophet *sallAllahu 'alayhi wa sallam*, his family, and his Companions *radhiAllahu 'anhum*, but it is important to control our love and other emotions, as excessive love can result in misguidance and misinterpretation of the teachings of Islam. The danger lies in falling into extremes, especially in having an overwhelming love for the Prophet *sallAllahu 'alayhi wa sallam's* family, as it can lead to deviations from the authentic teachings of the *Qur'an* and *Sunnah*. Therefore, our love and respect should be balanced, harmonious, and aligned with the teachings of Islam.

DID YOU KNOW?

Ibn 'Umar radhiAllahu 'anhu said, "We used to compare the people as to who was better at the time of the Messenger of Allah, sallAllahu 'alayhi wa sallam. We used to regard Abu Bakr as the best, then 'Umar ibn Al-Khattaab, then 'Uthman ibn 'Affaan radhiAllahu 'anhum." [49]

---

46 At-Tirmidhi
47 Sahih Muslim
48 They consider their *Imams* to be incapable of making errors or committing sins.
49 Sahih Al-Bukhari

SUMMARY: THE SHI'A

- Among the first sects that appeared in Islam.

- It emerged because of a disagreement over who should take leadership after the death of Prophet Muhammad *sallAllahu 'alayhi wa sallam*.

- They believe 'Ali ibn Abi Talib *radhiAllahu 'anhu*, should have been the first successor.

Among their core beliefs...

Their Imams are infallible, divinely appointed, and are responsible for the spiritual and political status of the Muslim community.

Emphasis on the concept of commemorating the martyrdom of Husayn *radhiAllahu 'anhu*.

Being extreme in their love for the Prophet *sallAllahu 'alayhi wa sallam*'s family, especially for 'Ali, Fatimah *radhiAllahu 'anhum*, and their descendants, who are revered as the Imams of the Shi'a. While they disrespect and curse other great Companions of the Prophet *sallAllahu 'alayhi wa sallam*.

Al-Bukhari & Muslim

Rejection of reports and statements of the Prophet *sallAllahu 'alayhi wa sallam* authenticated in *Sunni* sources like Al-Bukhari and Muslim.

UNIT 1 CHAPTERS 1-2

REVIEW AND REFLECT QUESTIONS

Based on what you have learned about the middle path, what would you do in the following situations?

1

You are invited to a youth program at a local *masjid*. Part of the program is on *tazkiyatun-nafs* (purification of the soul). You are asked to sit in a circle with other youth and engage in a form of *dhikr* by using the word *"Allah"* several times with emphasis on the end of the word *"hu"*. Should you participate in it? Explain the reason behind your decision.

2

You are invited to dinner. After dinner, you hear the host commenting, *"I only believe in the Qur'an and I don't believe in the hadith."* How would you respond to him?

3

You are visiting friends when you hear a mutual friend make the statement, *"I am a rational person, I don't believe if things don't make sense to me. I don't believe Allah has hands."* What would be the correct response to this statement?

4

You are invited to a gathering where a pious *Shaykh* is visiting from overseas. You enter the room and see the *Shaykh* seated in a chair where several people are greeting him by bending down and kissing his feet as a sign of respect. What would you do in this situation? Explain your decision.

CHAPTER 3

IS THIS REALLY ISLAM?

The emergence of Muslim sects primarily arises from internal differences, encompassing differences in both '*Aqeedah* and practices. However, there are certain sects within the Muslim community that have been influenced by ideologies that are external and unrelated to Islam. Despite their claims of adhering to Islamic principles and being integral to *Sunni* Islam, these sects have veered away from the authentic teachings of Islam.

These sects cannot even be recognized as Muslim due to their misguided beliefs. Their deviations, especially in matters concerning '*Aqeedah*, are so radical and distinct that they no longer fall within the framework of Islam. In the following section, we will explore some non-Muslim ideologies commonly associated with Islam, aiming to comprehend the reasons for their deviation and extract valuable lessons that guide us to stay steadfast on the true path.

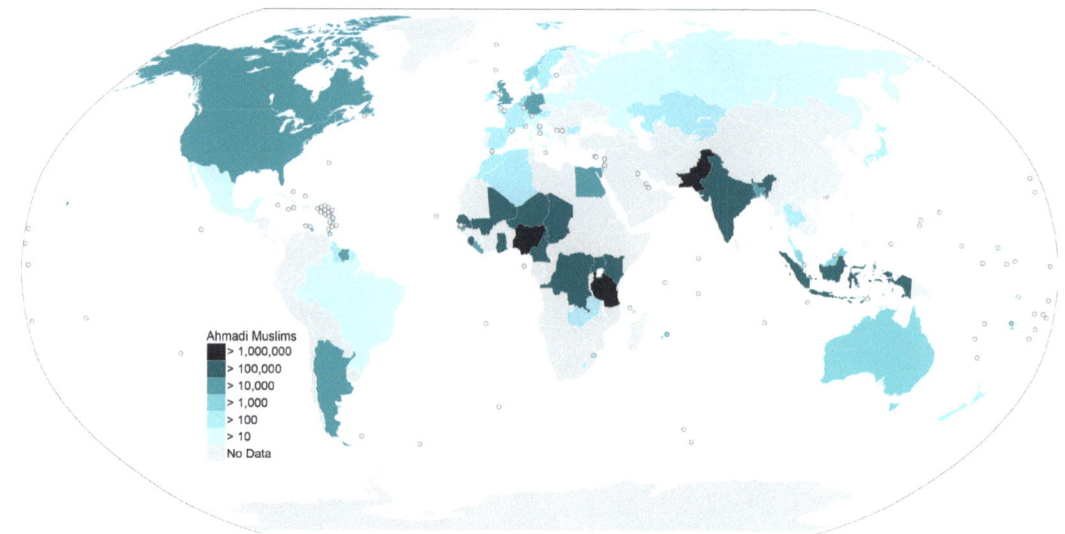

THE QADIYANI

The **Qadiyani** sect, also referred to as the **Ahmadiyyah** movement, originated during the late 19th century in Qadian, British India (now situated in present-day India). Established by Mirza Ghulam Ahmad (1835-1908).[50] This movement asserted his divine designation as a reformer, prophet, and the anticipated Messiah of several religions. The **Qadiyani** sect is predominantly concentrated in the Indian subcontinent, including India, Bangladesh, and Pakistan, though its adherents span across global regions.

HISTORY OF THE QADIYANI

In 1889, Mirza Ghulam Ahmad, the originator of the **Qadiyani** sect, publicly announced that he had received revelations directly from Allah. These divine messages guided his mission to reform Islam and bring together all monotheistic religious communities under the umbrella of Islam. He assumed the mantle of a prophet, identifying himself as the **Mahdi** (the guided one) and the Messiah, thereby fulfilling prophecies from diverse religious traditions. This proclamation garnered a following in **Qadian**, and over time, his influence expanded to attract adherents from various regions of the Indian subcontinent and beyond.

However, the assertion of prophethood of Mirza Ghulam Ahmad and his claim of divine revelations gave rise to controversies and opposition from established Islamic scholars. The crux of the matter rested on his divergence from *Sunni* Islamic teachings, with the majority of scholars rejecting his claims. They argued that the doctrine of the finality of Prophethood, a fundamental traditional Islamic belief, upheld that no prophet or messenger would emerge after Prophet Muhammad, *sallAllahu 'alayhi wa sallam*.

50 Encyclopedia Britannica

BELIEFS OF THE QADIYANI

The *Qadiyani* sect holds some unique beliefs that set them apart from *Sunni* Islam. One significant difference is their belief in Mirza Ghulam Ahmad as a prophet, which goes against traditional Islamic teachings. Another notable feature is their strong allegiance to a *khalifah* who follows Mirza Ghulam Ahmad. These beliefs trace back to Mirza Ghulam Ahmad's claims of receiving divine messages and his role as the *Mahdi* sent to revive Islam. He even went so far as to claim a connection with the Hindu avatar Krishna, considering him a prophet too. They also have a distinct perspective on bearing arms; they believe that Muslims should not bear arms, even in self-defense. Some speculate that this stance might have been influenced by British control over India, possibly aimed at promoting a servile acceptance of imperialism. These differences in beliefs have led to the exclusion of *Qadiyanis* from *Sunni* Islam.

CLAIM OF PROPHETHOOD

Let's examine the claim of prophethood in this context. Once we address and successfully disprove this assertion, it will become apparent that the entire belief system of this sect lacks a foundation, rendering it incompatible with the principles of Islam.

A central point within the *Qadiyani* sect lies in their rejection of Prophet Muhammad *sallAllahu 'alayhi wa sallam* as the final messenger. Instead, they believe that Mirza Ghulam Ahmad is also a prophet, not to introduce new religious practices but to reaffirm and endorse the beliefs of Islam. Furthermore, others within this sect claim he is the anticipated *Mahdi*. Nonetheless, this assertion can be easily debunked, as it directly contradicts the words of Allah.

Allah tells us,

مَّا كَانَ مُحَمَّدٌ أَبَآ أَحَدٍ مِّن رِّجَالِكُمْ وَلَٰكِن رَّسُولَ ٱللَّهِ وَخَاتَمَ ٱلنَّبِيِّۦنَ وَكَانَ ٱللَّهُ بِكُلِّ شَىْءٍ عَلِيمًا

"Muhammad is not the father of [any] one of your men, but [he is] the Messenger of Allah and last of the prophets. And ever is Allah, of all things, Knowing." [51]

Upon examining the **hadiths** of the Prophet *sallAllahu 'alayhi wa sallam*, we discover several instances that contradict this assertion. For example, during the expedition to Tabuk, the Prophet *sallAllahu 'alayhi wa sallam* entrusted 'Ali *radhiAllahu 'anhu* with leadership responsibilities. 'Ali *radhiAllahu 'anhu* said,

"O Allah's Messenger sallAllahu 'alayhi wa sallam, are you leaving me behind amongst women and children? Thereupon he (the Prophet sallAllahu 'alayhi wa sallam) said: "Aren't you satisfied with being unto me what Haroon was unto Musa but with this exception that there would be no prophet after me." [52]

This **hadith** shows that the connection between the Prophet *sallAllahu 'alayhi wa sallam* and 'Ali *radhiAllahu 'anhu,* is akin to that of Musa and Haroon *'alayhimus salaam*. In this analogy, 'Ali *radhiAllahu 'anhu* plays a role similar to Haroon alongside Musa *'alayhimus salaam*, offering support and assistance to

---

51 Surah Al-Ahzaab [33:40]
52 Sahih Muslim

Prophet Muhammad sallAllahu 'alayhi wa sallam. In another *hadith*, the Prophet sallAllahu 'alayhi wa sallam shared a comparison between himself and other prophets.

He sallAllahu 'alayhi wa sallam said, *"The parable of myself and the Prophets is that of a man who built a house and did a complete and good job, except for the space of one brick. Whoever entered it would look at that space and say how good it is, apart from the space of that brick. My position is like that of that brick, and the Prophets 'alayhimus salaam end with me."* [53]

Ibn Katheer's commentary on the aforementioned *ayah* in *Surah Al-Ahzaab*, reinforces the finality of Prophet Muhammad's sallAllahu 'alayhi wa sallam. He concludes with the following statement: *"Allah has told us in His Book, and His Messenger sallAllahu 'alayhi wa sallam has told us in the Mutawatir Sunnah,* [54] *that there will be no Prophet after him, so that it may be known that everyone who claims this status after him is a liar and fabricator who is misguided and is misguiding others. Even if he twists meanings, comes up with false claims, and uses tricks and vagaries, all of this is false and is misguidance, as will be clear to those who have understanding."* [55]

The *Qadiyani* sect takes a significant detour by rejecting the core belief that Prophet Muhammad sallAllahu 'alayhi wa sallam, serves as the final messenger. These deviations steer them away from true Islamic beliefs, resulting in their exclusion from the Muslim community at large. This highlights the importance of not only accepting and adhering to the *Qur'an* and *Sunnah* but also ensuring our adherence follows the understanding of the Prophet sallAllahu 'alayhi wa sallam, and the first generations of believers. These early followers possess deep insights into the genuine essence and significance of the *Qur'an* and *Sunnah*, making their interpretation highly valuable, thereby safeguarding us from falling into these types of sects and misguidance.

---

53 Sahih Muslim

54 ***Mutawatir Sunnah*** is a *sunnah* that was conveyed by numerous narrators that it is not possible that they agreed upon an untruth.

55 Tafseer Ibn Katheer

> ### DID YOU KNOW?
>
> *The Prophet sallAllahu 'alayhi wa sallam said,*
>
> *"In my nation, there will be twenty-seven great liars and impostors, among whom are four women. Verily, I am the seal of the prophets, and there is no prophet after me."*[56]

THE NATION OF ISLAM

The **Nation of Islam** (NOI) is a religious sect and movement that emerged in the United States during the early 20th century. It is a distinct sect that claims adherence to Islam. It professes a blend of Islamic doctrines with Black nationalist concepts and principles of social reform, alongside elements of Christianity. Guided by charismatic figures, the Nation of Islam has played a significant role in advocating for the rights and empowerment of African Americans and promoting a sect that claims adherence to Islam.

HISTORY OF THE NATION OF ISLAM

The Nation of Islam sect was founded in 1930 by Wallace Fard Muhammad, who taught that he was the **Mahdi**[57] (guided one) and the long-awaited Messiah.[58] Fard Muhammad's teachings blended elements of Islam, Christianity, and black nationalist ideologies. He attracted a following primarily in urban African American communities, especially in cities like Detroit and Chicago.

After the mysterious disappearance of Fard Muhammad, the leadership of the Nation of Islam passed to Elijah Muhammad, who became its most prominent and influential leader. Under Elijah Muhammad's leadership, the Nation of Islam grew significantly and gained attention for its emphasis on Black pride, self-reliance, and separatism.

---

56 Ahmad

57 The *Mahdi* is mentioned in *hadith* as a Rightly-Guided leader who will appear at the end of times to rid the world of evil and injustice. The Prophet *sallAllahu 'alayhi wa sallam* said, *"The Mahdi is one of us, a member of my family. Allah will guide him in a single night."* (Ahmad)

58 In Islam, the *Qur'an* identifies the true Messiah as 'Isa *'alayhis salaam*. Allah says, *"...The Messiah, Jesus the son of Mary, was but a messenger of Allah..."* (*Surah An-Nisaa'* 4:171).

One of the most famous figures associated with the Nation of Islam was Malcolm X, also known as El-Hajj Malik El-Shabazz. Malcolm X's fiery speeches and advocacy for Black empowerment made him a prominent spokesperson for the movement. However, his relationship with the Nation of Islam became strained, and he eventually left the organization to pursue *Sunni* Islam.

After the death of Elijah Muhammad in 1975, his son Warith Deen Mohammed became the leader and moved the organization towards *Sunni* Islam. He disavowed many of the controversial beliefs and practices of the Nation of Islam, leading to the transformation of a large portion of its followers into *Sunni* Islam.

Despite these changes, a small sect of the Nation of Islam under Louis Farrakhan retained its original teachings and separatist stance. This branch continues to exist as a separate entity with a focus on African American empowerment and the promotion of its beliefs and practices, claiming adherence to Islam.

BELIEFS OF THE NATION OF ISLAM

The Nation of Islam sect holds a number of deviant beliefs that set them apart from *Sunni* Islam. Among these beliefs is their belief that Allah incarnated as a Black man, and some further believe the idea that their founder, Wallace Fard Muhammad, embodied the divine and was Allah. Additionally, they hold the belief that Elijah Muhammad was a prophet and also the embodiment of Prophet 'Isa *'alayhis salaam*. As for Prophet Muhammad *sallAllahu 'alayhi wa sallam*, they hold the view that He *sallAllahu 'alayhi wa sallam* was sent solely to the Arabs and that Allah sent Elijah Muhammad to lead the African-American community, considering him the "savior" and the final messenger. [59]

---

59   *Al-Mawsoo'ah Al-Muyassarah fil-Madhaahib wal-Adyaan Al-Mu'aasirah*

THE LORDSHIP OF ALLAH

The concept of Allah's Lordship, known as **Ar-Ruboobiyyah**, revolves around the belief that Allah is the Creator, Sustainer, Owner, and Maintainer of all that is in existence. His complete authority spans from the smallest particles to the grandest stars and planets. This belief offers insight into the immense greatness of Allah, who not only provides for us and cares for us but also manages and oversees the entirety of the universe. Regrettably, there are those like the Nation of Islam sect who reject this. They not only disregard proper worship of Allah but also question Allah's Lordship, holding beliefs such as assigning human qualities to Allah or asserting His descent in human form.

Allah tells us,

ٱلَّذِى لَهُۥ مُلْكُ ٱلسَّمَٰوَٰتِ وَٱلْأَرْضِ وَلَمْ يَتَّخِذْ وَلَدًا وَلَمْ يَكُن لَّهُۥ شَرِيكٌ فِى ٱلْمُلْكِ وَخَلَقَ كُلَّ شَىْءٍ فَقَدَّرَهُۥ تَقْدِيرًا وَٱتَّخَذُوا مِن دُونِهِۦ ءَالِهَةً لَّا يَخْلُقُونَ شَيْئًا وَهُمْ يُخْلَقُونَ وَلَا يَمْلِكُونَ لِأَنفُسِهِمْ ضَرًّا وَلَا نَفْعًا وَلَا يَمْلِكُونَ مَوْتًا وَلَا حَيَوٰةً وَلَا نُشُورًا

"He to whom belongs the dominion of the heavens and the earth and who has not taken a son and has not had a partner in dominion and has created each thing and determined it with [precise] determination. But they have taken besides Him gods which create nothing, while they are created, and possess not for themselves any harm or benefit and possess not [power to cause] death or life or resurrection." [60]

---

60 Surah Al-Furqaan [25:2-3]

In another *ayah* of the *Qur'an*, Allah not only asserts that Prophet Muhammad *sallAllahu 'alayhi wa sallam* is the messenger for all of humanity, but also reinforces the *tawheed* of Allah. Allah tells us,

قُلْ يَٰٓأَيُّهَا ٱلنَّاسُ إِنِّى رَسُولُ ٱللَّهِ إِلَيْكُمْ جَمِيعًا ٱلَّذِى لَهُۥ مُلْكُ ٱلسَّمَٰوَٰتِ وَٱلْأَرْضِ لَآ إِلَٰهَ إِلَّا هُوَ يُحْىِۦ وَيُمِيتُ فَـَٔامِنُوا۟ بِٱللَّهِ وَرَسُولِهِ ٱلنَّبِىِّ ٱلْأُمِّىِّ ٱلَّذِى يُؤْمِنُ بِٱللَّهِ وَكَلِمَٰتِهِۦ وَٱتَّبِعُوهُ لَعَلَّكُمْ تَهْتَدُونَ

"Say, [O Muhammad], "O mankind, indeed I am the Messenger of Allah to you all, [from Him] to whom belongs the dominion of the heavens and the earth. There is no deity except Him; He gives life and causes death." So believe in Allah and His Messenger, the unlettered prophet, who believes in Allah and His words, and follow him that you may be guided." [61]

Having a strong and accurate grasp of the *Qur'an* and *Sunnah* is really important. It helps us identify weaknesses in the beliefs of different groups, like The Nation of Islam, by using evidence from the *Qur'an* and *Sunnah*. This highlights why it's crucial to stick closely to the teachings of the *Qur'an* to stay on the right path and avoid going astray. It's worth knowing that, as time has passed, most of The Nation of Islam's followers have shifted towards *Sunni* Islam. Only a small group, led by Louis Farrakhan, still hold on to their different beliefs.

---

61   Surah Al-A'raaf [7:158]

BRAIN TEASER

TEST YOUR KNOWLEDGE

1. Identify a group that believes in a false prophet.

2. Identify a group that believes committing major sins takes you out of the fold of Islam.

3. Identify a group that believes it is ok to insult a Companion of the Prophet *sallAllahu 'alayhi wa sallam*.

4. Identify a group that denies the *Sunnah*.

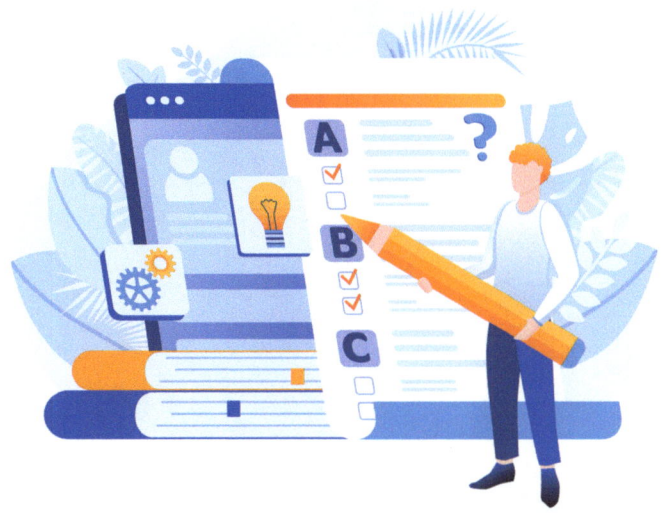

UNIT 1 CHAPTER 3
REVIEW AND REFLECT QUESTIONS

1
What major similarity do both *Qadiyanis* and the Nation of Islam share?

2
Which two *ayaat* in the *Qur'an* clearly indicate that the Prophet *sallAllahu 'alayhi wa sallam* is the final Prophet and he *sallAllahu 'alayhi wa sallam* was sent for all of mankind to follow?

3
Research and write a paragraph on the rationale behind Malcolm X's shift from the Nation of Islam to *Sunni* Islam.

4
Why is it not permitted to pray behind a *Qadiyani* or follower of the Nation of Islam?

UNIT 2
COMMON DEVIATIONS

UNIT 2

IMPORTANT VOCABULARY

AHLUL-KITAAB
People of the Book; refers to the Jews and the Christians whom Allah revealed Scriptures.

AGNOSTICISM
The belief that it is not possible to know whether God exists or not.

ATHEISM
The belief that God or gods do not exist.

BUDDHISM
A religion widely followed in Asia, based on the teaching of Buddha.

CHRISTIANITY
The religion that is based on the teachings of Jesus Christ and the belief that he was the son of God.

DEEN
Religion; a complete way of life.

DEISM
The belief in God based on reason rather than revelation or the teaching of any specific religion.

HINDUISM
The main religion of India which includes the worship of one or more gods and the belief in reincarnation.

INJEEL
The Gospel of 'Isa 'alayhis salaam.

JUDAISM
The religion of the Jewish people, based mainly on the first five books of the Bible and the Talmud.

KARMA
Hindu and Bhuddist belief that somebody's good and bad actions in one of their lives will decide what will happen to them in their next life.

TRINITY
Trinity is the term to signify the central doctrine of the Christian religion. Their belief that in One Godhead exists three persons; the Father, the Son, and the Holy Spirit.

TABLE OF CONTENTS

UNIT 2 | COMMON DEVIATIONS

CHAPTER	PG	
04	57	INTRODUCTION
05	61	CHRISTIANITY & JUDAISM
06	73	HINDUISM & BUDDHISM
07	81	DEISM, AGNOSTICISM, & ATHEISM

ESSENTIAL QUESTIONS

This unit is designed to help answer the following questions.

1. Why is it important to know the history of other world religions and ideologies?
2. What lessons can we learn from other religions?
3. How does change occur in a religion over time?
4. What do the similarities in Judaism, Christianity, and Islam prove?

CHAPTER 4

INTRODUCTION

In the next chapters, we will explore some world religions and common non-Muslim ideologies. We will embark on a journey to better understand the world's diverse religions and ideologies, looking into their unique beliefs, worship, spirituality, and their specific beliefs about the Day of Judgment. We will briefly examine religions like Christianity, Judaism, Hinduism, and Buddhism. We will also look at other beliefs and ideologies such as Deism, Agnosticism, and Atheism. By briefly looking into each of these, we aim to better understand their beliefs while also making comparisons to the one true **deen** (a complete way of life), Islam.

DID YOU KNOW?

There is only one true religion. Many people today claim to follow various religions and spiritual paths. You find people from all corners of the world claiming that their way is the true path. Christians claim that only those who accept 'Isa *alayhis salaam* as their Lord and Savior will enter paradise. Jews claim that only Jews who are the chosen people will enter paradise. And every group claims similar beliefs. So who is right? How do we know which is the right path?

Any religious scriptural source must meet certain criteria to be considered as true. Firstly, the origin must be traceable. Secondly, the original text should be preserved and unchanged. Thirdly, the information contained within it must be accurate or factual. Finally, if predictions or statements about the future have been proven correct, it

is a clear indication of divine origin because human beings are simply unable to know the future with complete accuracy on their own. The sources of other religions have been proven to be tampered with by humans. This has resulted in several versions of the original texts. Islam, on the other hand, is the only divinely guided religion whose original sources are impeccably preserved and meet the criteria of verification. Islam is the one true path, and this claim is directly from Allah.

Allah tells us,

إِنَّ ٱلدِّينَ عِندَ ٱللَّهِ ٱلْإِسْلَٰمُ وَمَا ٱخْتَلَفَ ٱلَّذِينَ أُوتُوا۟ ٱلْكِتَٰبَ إِلَّا مِنۢ بَعْدِ مَا جَآءَهُمُ ٱلْعِلْمُ بَغْيًۢا بَيْنَهُمْ وَمَن يَكْفُرْ بِـَٔايَٰتِ ٱللَّهِ فَإِنَّ ٱللَّهَ سَرِيعُ ٱلْحِسَابِ

"Certainly, Allah's only Way is Islam. Those who were given the Scripture did not dispute (among themselves) out of mutual envy until knowledge came to them. Whoever denies Allah's signs, then surely Allah is swift in reckoning." [62]

---

62 Surah Ale-'Imraan [3:19]

CHAPTER 5

JUDAISM & CHRISTIANITY

JUDAISM

Judaism, one of the world's oldest religions, has a rich history spanning over two thousand years. Its roots can be traced back to Ibrahim, Ishaq, and Ya'qub *'alayhis salaam*. According to Jewish sources, Ibrahim *'alayhis salaam* was born in the city of Ur in Babylon in the year 1800 BCE. [63] He was the son of Terach, an idol merchant. He lived his early life questioning the belief in idol worship, which eventually led him to believe in a single God and creator.

Eventually, the one true God that Ibrahim *'alayhis salaam* had worshiped called to him and made him a covenant: if Ibrahim *'alayhis salaam* would leave his home and his people, then God would make him a great nation and bless him. Ibrahim *'alayhis salaam* accepted this covenant, and this became the foundation of the Jewish people being the chosen people of God.

Ibrahim *'alayhis salaam* married Sarah, who was not able to bear children, so she gave her slave Hagar to Ibrahim *'alayhis salaam*, and Hagar conceived Isma'il *'alayhis salaam*. Later,

---

63   Before Common Era or Before Christian Era: used when referring to a year before the birth of Jesus when the Christian calendar starts counting years.

God revealed to Ibrahim that Sarah would also give birth to their son, Ishaq 'alayhis salaam. Ishaq 'alayhis salaam later had a son named Ya'qub 'alayhis salaam, and from him descended the Children of Israel.

Ya'qub 'alayhis salaam, also known as Israel, holds a significant place in the history of the Children of Israel. He was the father of twelve sons, each of whom became a leader of one of the twelve tribes within the community. Together, they lived in the land of Palestine, marking the roots of this ancient lineage. However, one of Ya'qub's 'alayhis salaam sons, Yusuf 'alayhis salaam, played a particularly compelling role in their history. His story, shared in both the *Qur'an* and the Bible, is one of betrayal and resilience.

Yusuf 'alayhis salaam was tragically betrayed and sold into slavery by his own brothers, an event that altered the course of his life dramatically. His journey led him to Egypt, where he confronted numerous trials and challenges. Through divine wisdom and guidance, Yusuf 'alayhis salaam eventually ascended to a position of immense influence in Egypt. His policies and insight became instrumental in saving Egypt and its neighboring regions from a crippling famine. This pivotal role led to a heartfelt reunion with his brothers, who came to Egypt, settled there, and ultimately reunited with their father, Ya'qub 'alayhis salaam, shaping a crucial chapter in the history of the Children of Israel.

The Children of Israel lived in Egypt until the time of the Pharaohs. It was during that time that they endured severe persecution and enslavement. This oppression and injustice reached such an extent that the Pharaohs issued orders for the killing of newborns among the Children of Israel. It is believed that Musa 'alayhis salaam was born during this period.

The story of Musa 'alayhis salaam and Pharaoh's confrontation is found both in the *Qur'an* and the Bible. Musa 'alayhis salaam ultimately achieved victory over Pharaoh, leading his people out of Egypt and into the desert. However, instead of following Allah's command to enter the Holy Land, the Children of Israel hesitated and refused to obey and ended up wandering lost in the desert.

The children of Israel eventually entered the land that is today Palestine and lived there for many centuries to come. From time to time, they were conquered by different empires, which often led to their exile, scattering them to various parts of the world. This is why you can find Jewish communities in many regions, including Europe, North Africa, and even the Middle East.

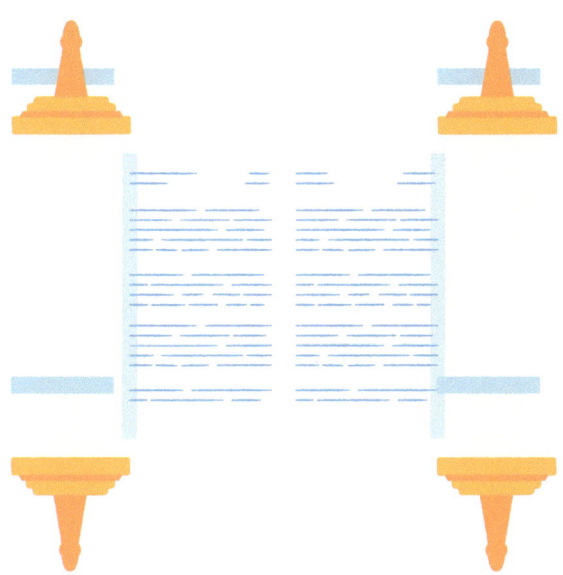

JEWISH BELIEFS

Judaism, a monotheistic religion, is characterized by a set of core beliefs deeply rooted in the Torah. One of these foundational beliefs is monotheism, wherein Jews affirm the absolute oneness of God, often referred to as *Yahweh* or *Adonai*.

This monotheistic principle is central to their faith and is expressed in their declaration of faith: *"Hear, O Israel: The Lord our God, the Lord is one."* This belief in the oneness of God aligns with the concept of monotheism and resonates with our belief as Muslims as well. That is why it is not uncommon to find Jews who feel comfortable worshiping God in a mosque, as they share a belief in the singular nature of God, while they may be more hesitant to do so in a church, as they perceive it as endorsing practices associated with idol worship.

Allah addresses the **Ahlul-Kitaab** (People of the Book) [64] in the following *ayah*,

قُلْ يَٰٓأَهْلَ ٱلْكِتَٰبِ تَعَالَوْا۟ إِلَىٰ كَلِمَةٍ سَوَآءٍۭ بَيْنَنَا وَبَيْنَكُمْ أَلَّا نَعْبُدَ إِلَّا ٱللَّهَ وَلَا نُشْرِكَ بِهِۦ شَيْـًٔا وَلَا يَتَّخِذَ بَعْضُنَا بَعْضًا أَرْبَابًۭا مِّن دُونِ ٱللَّهِ فَإِن تَوَلَّوْا۟ فَقُولُوا۟ ٱشْهَدُوا۟ بِأَنَّا مُسْلِمُونَ

"Say, "O People of the Scripture, come to a word that is equitable between us and you - that we will not worship except Allah and not associate anything with Him and not take one another as lords instead of Allah." But if they turn away, then say, "Bear witness that we are Muslims (submitting to Him)."" [65]

---

64 *Ahlul-Kitaab* refers to the Jews and the Christians to whom Allah sent messengers and scriptures.
65 Surah Ale-'Imraan [3:64]

DID YOU KNOW?

WHO ARE "AHLUL-KITAAB"?

Ahlul-Kitaab refers to the Jews and the Christians to whom Allah sent messengers and scriptures. In English, they are called the *"People of the Book."* The *Qur'an* refers to them as *Ahlul-Kitaab* because of the books that were sent to them by Allah. The Torah was sent to Musa *'alayhis salaam* for the Jews, while the *Injeel* (Gospel) was sent to Isa *'alayhis salaam*.

Muslims are encouraged to treat the *Ahlul-Kitaab* with respect and fairness. Allah has mentioned their special status in contrast to other religions and ideologies by mentioning in the *Qur'an* that their food (i.e., meat) can be eaten by Muslims, and Muslim men are allowed to marry chaste women from the "People of the Book." [66]

---

66 There are details regarding marrying **Ahlul-Kitaab** mentioned in Islamic jurisprudence. Scholars have established certain conditions and requirements for pursuing such a marriage.

ISLAMIC VIEWPOINT

While Judaism and Islam indeed share many commonalities in their beliefs and practices, there exist differences between them, particularly regarding the concept of the Day of Judgment and the afterlife. In Islam, the belief in the Day of Judgment is fundamental and is a pillar of *iman*. This belief is emphasized in many *ayaat* and *hadiths*. Belief in the Day of Judgment means individuals are judged by Allah about their deeds and will be rewarded or punished accordingly.

On the other hand, many Jews do not believe in the concept of an afterlife, heaven, or hell. It's important to note that within Judaism, beliefs regarding the afterlife are diverse and many. While some Jewish traditions do include a belief in an afterlife, others place greater emphasis on the present life and moral living in this world.

While Judaism and Islam share similar historic roots, beliefs, and practices, it is important to acknowledge that if they are both from the same source, then we must also believe that the later revelation is to be followed and abrogates the earlier. Allah tells us,

وَأَنزَلْنَآ إِلَيْكَ ٱلْكِتَٰبَ بِٱلْحَقِّ مُصَدِّقًا لِّمَا بَيْنَ يَدَيْهِ مِنَ ٱلْكِتَٰبِ وَمُهَيْمِنًا عَلَيْهِ

"And We have revealed to you, [O Muhammad], the Book in truth, confirming that which preceded it of the Scripture and as a criterion over it." [67]

---

67 Surah Al-Ma'idah [5:48]

And it is reported from Prophet Muhammad *sallAllahu 'alayhi wa sallam* that he said:

"Jabir said that when 'Umar came to the Prophet sallAllahu 'alayhi wa sallam saying, "We hear from Jews traditions that charm us, so do you think we should write down some of them?" He sallAllahu 'alayhi wa sallam replied, "Are you in a state of confusion as the Jews and the Christians were? I have brought them to you white and pure, **and if Musa were alive he would feel it absolutely necessary to follow me."** [68]

CHRISTIANITY

Christianity, one of the world's largest religions, has a long and interesting history, starting around the 1st century CE [69] within the Roman Empire and in a region that corresponds to present-day Palestine. At the heart of its historical background lies the life and teachings of Isa *'alayhis salaam*, also known as Jesus Christ in the western world. 'Isa *'alayhis salaam* is considered the central figure and Messiah of the Christian religion. He was born around 4 BCE in a village called Bethlehem; however, his early life was mostly in the village of Nazareth. Not much is known about the early history of 'Isa *'alayhis salaam* until his 30s, when he embarked on a journey of teaching. His message centered on compassion and love for one another.

From the beginning, he was betrayed and judged by the Jews to be a heretic since he was originally a Jew. After some time, he was sentenced by the Roman authorities to death by crucifixion.

The crucifixion of 'Isa *'alayhis salaam*, estimated to have occurred between 30 and 33 CE, is a very important historical time for Christians and also marked a pivotal moment in Christian history. According to Christian beliefs, this event served as an atoning sacrifice, offering redemption and forgiveness of sins to humanity. This Christian belief in the resurrection holds that 'Isa *'alayhis salaam* rose from the dead three days after his crucifixion, affirming his divine status and the promise of eternal life. Following 'Isa's *'alayhis salaam* ascension into heaven, his disciples played an important role in spreading his teachings throughout the Roman Empire and beyond.

By the 4th century CE, under the rule of Emperor Constantine, Christianity was

---

68   *Mishkat Al-Masabih* is a selection of **hadith** compiled by Imam At-Tabrizi (d. 741 AH)
69   CE is an abbreviation for Common Era or Christian Era. It means the same as AD (Anno Domini) and represents the start of the calendar from the approximate birth of Jesus.

officially recognized and became the official religion of the Roman Empire. Constantine's conversion to Christianity and the Edict of Milan in 313 CE marked a historic shift, allowing Christians to practice their faith openly and eventually leading to the First Council of Nicaea in 325 CE, where important theological doctrines were established. This period of consolidation and growth laid the foundation for the diverse Christian traditions and denominations seen today. [70]

After the collapse of the Roman Empire, Christianity split into many different sects and branches, like the Eastern Orthodox and Catholicism. These strands of Christianity over time split even further, causing the different denominations and churches. Christianity spread across the world, mainly due to Christian missionary work and Europe's colonization of many parts of the world.

CHRISTIAN BELIEFS

Christianity, with its diverse and numerous denominations and interpretations, is unified by certain beliefs that form the foundation of the Christian religion. These beliefs are mainly rooted in the teachings of 'Isa *alayhis salaam* and are central to Christian belief.

Christianity firmly claims that it is monotheistic, affirming the existence of one God. This belief is shared by Judaism and Islam in acknowledging the absolute oneness of God. However, Christianity distinguishes itself by the concept of the Trinity, which consists of God the Father, God the Son, and God the Holy Spirit. This belief in the triune God is specific to Christianity, setting it apart from other monotheistic religions. Their belief in the Trinity actually corrupts their monotheism, since that belief leads them to worship others besides God. As we see today, many Christians worship and recognize 'Isa *alayhis salaam* as God and even attribute to him things He himself never taught. Islam strictly adheres to the belief in the absolute oneness of Allah, with no partners or associates. Our belief rejects the concept of the Trinity, as it is a belief that God is divisible and no longer unique or one, and this belief is incompatible with the pure *tawheed* taught in the *Qur'an*. Allah says,

وَإِلَٰهُكُمْ إِلَٰهٌ وَٰحِدٌ لَّا إِلَٰهَ إِلَّا هُوَ ٱلرَّحْمَٰنُ ٱلرَّحِيمُ

***"And your god is one God**. There is no deity [worthy of worship] except Him, the Entirely Merciful, the Especially Merciful."* [71]

---

70   Bernard J. Mcginn, John Hick, "Christianity," Britannica.com, December 5, 2024, https://www.britannica.com/topic/Christianity
71   Surah Al-Baqarah [2:163]

In another *ayah* Allah tells us,

قُلْ يَـٰٓأَهْلَ ٱلْكِتَـٰبِ تَعَالَوْا۟ إِلَىٰ كَلِمَةٍۢ سَوَآءٍۭ بَيْنَنَا وَبَيْنَكُمْ أَلَّا نَعْبُدَ إِلَّا ٱللَّهَ وَلَا نُشْرِكَ بِهِۦ شَيْـًۭٔا وَلَا يَتَّخِذَ بَعْضُنَا بَعْضًا أَرْبَابًۭا مِّن دُونِ ٱللَّهِ ۚ فَإِن تَوَلَّوْا۟ فَقُولُوا۟ ٱشْهَدُوا۟ بِأَنَّا مُسْلِمُونَ

"Say, "O People of the Scripture, come to a word that is equitable between us and you - that we will not worship except Allah and not associate anything with Him and not take one another as lords instead of Allah ." But if they turn away, then say, "Bear witness that we are Muslims [submitting to Him]." [72]

NOT ALL CHRISTIANS ARE THE SAME

Not all early Christians shared the same beliefs about 'Isa *alayhis salaam* being divine. The emperor Constantine convened The First Council of Nicaea, held in 325 AD, in order to unify Christian beliefs. This council resulted in the creation of the Nicene Creed, one of the most significant statements of Christian faith in history. This council was convened to address theological disputes within Christianity, particularly the controversy surrounding the nature of 'Isa *alayhis salaam*. The council concluded with the Nicene Creed, which affirmed the doctrine of the Trinity, declaring that 'Isa *alayhis salaam* is "of the same substance" as God the Father, a concept that played a crucial role in shaping Christian theology and beliefs for centuries to come. The Nicene Creed continues to be followed today by various denominations of Christianity. [73]

CHRISTIAN BELIEF ON CRUCIFIXION

Another belief of Christianity is the crucifixion of 'Isa *alayhis salaam*. Christians believe that 'Isa *alayhis salaam* is the son of God and the savior of mankind. Christians believe that 'Isa *alayhis salaam* was crucified and then rose from the dead; according to them, this provided a means of salvation for humanity. By accepting 'Isa *alayhis salaam* as Lord and believing in his crucifixion and redemption, anyone can attain forgiveness of sins and the promise of eternal life in paradise. This belief in salvation through 'Isa *alayhis salaam* is a central pillar of Christian belief. However, this belief is problematic and rejected by other monotheistic religions like Judaism and Islam. This belief essentially means that people will not be accountable for their actions as long as they accept 'Isa *alayhis salaam* having died on the cross for their sins. In Islam, everyone will be accountable for their own deeds, and no soul shall take the burden of another.

---

[72] Surah Ale-'Imraan [3:64]
[73] The Editors of Encyclopedia Britannica, "First Council of Nicaea, Christianity [325]." Britannica.com, November 29, 2024, https://www.britannica.com/event/First-Council-of-Nicaea-325

Allah says,

مَّنِ ٱهْتَدَىٰ فَإِنَّمَا يَهْتَدِى لِنَفْسِهِۦ وَمَن ضَلَّ فَإِنَّمَا يَضِلُّ عَلَيْهَا وَلَا تَزِرُ وَازِرَةٌ وِزْرَ أُخْرَىٰ وَمَا كُنَّا مُعَذِّبِينَ حَتَّىٰ نَبْعَثَ رَسُولًا

"Whoever is guided is only guided for [the benefit of] his soul. And whoever errs only errs against it. And no bearer of burdens will bear the burden of another. And never would We punish until We sent a messenger." [74]

As for the crucifixion, Muslims do not believe that 'Isa *'alayhis salaam* was crucified and died on the cross. Muslims believe that Allah lifted him up. Allah tells us,

وَقَوْلِهِمْ إِنَّا قَتَلْنَا ٱلْمَسِيحَ عِيسَى ٱبْنَ مَرْيَمَ رَسُولَ ٱللَّهِ وَمَا قَتَلُوهُ وَمَا صَلَبُوهُ وَلَٰكِن شُبِّهَ لَهُمْ وَإِنَّ ٱلَّذِينَ ٱخْتَلَفُوا فِيهِ لَفِى شَكٍّ مِّنْهُ مَا لَهُم بِهِۦ مِنْ عِلْمٍ إِلَّا ٱتِّبَاعَ ٱلظَّنِّ وَمَا قَتَلُوهُ يَقِينًۢا بَل رَّفَعَهُ ٱللَّهُ إِلَيْهِ وَكَانَ ٱللَّهُ عَزِيزًا حَكِيمًا

"And [for] their saying, "Indeed, we have killed the Messiah, Jesus, the son of Mary, the messenger of Allah." And they did not kill him, nor did they crucify him; but [another] was made to resemble him to them. And indeed, those who differ over it are in doubt about it. They have no knowledge of it except the following of assumption. And they did not kill him, for certain. Rather, Allah raised him to Himself. And ever is Allah Exalted in Might and Wise." [75]

THE BIBLE IN CHRISTIAN BELIEF

Another fundamental belief is that the Bible is sacred scripture, and some even claim it is the literal word of God. The current Bible consists of two main sections: the Old Testament and the New Testament. The Old Testament contains writings that are also recognized by Judaism, while the New Testament contains writings that specifically pertain to the life, teachings, and early history of Christianity.

Key books in the New Testament include the Gospels (Matthew, Mark, Luke, and John), which document the life and teachings of 'Isa *'alayhis salaam* and provide guidance to early Christian communities. It is important to know that the four Gospels mentioned above are not the only ones in existence; there are many other Gospels that are not included in the Bible.

---

74 Surah Al-Israa' [17:15]

75 Surah An-Nisaa' [4:157-158]

ISLAMIC VIEWPOINT

As Muslims, one of our core beliefs is the belief in books. We believe Allah sent down scriptures to his messengers, *'alayhumus salaam*. And for that reason, we affirm that 'Isa *'alayhis salaam* was teaching the **Injeel** [76] and that the current Bible, which includes the Gospels, was written after the life of Isa *'alayhis salaam*. We believe that Allah sent down the *Injeel* to 'Isa *'alayhis salaam* just as He sent down the *Qur'an* to Prophet Muhammad *sallAllahu 'alayhi wa sallam* and the Torah to Musa *'alayhis salaam*. However, it is important to know that the *Qur'an* abrogates all previous scriptures and that mankind is obligated to follow the last messenger, Muhammad *sallAllahu 'alayhi wa sallam*.

WAS 'ISA ' ALAYHIS SALAAM CRUCIFIED?

Unlike the Christian view of the death of 'Isa *'alayhis salaam*, Muslims believe 'Isa *'alayhis salaam* was raised to Heaven without being put on the cross, and Allah created a resemblance to appear exactly like him who was crucified in his place. Allah tells us in the *Qur'an*,

وَقَوْلِهِمْ إِنَّا قَتَلْنَا ٱلْمَسِيحَ عِيسَى ٱبْنَ مَرْيَمَ رَسُولَ ٱللَّهِ وَمَا قَتَلُوهُ وَمَا صَلَبُوهُ وَلَـٰكِن شُبِّهَ لَهُمْ وَإِنَّ ٱلَّذِينَ ٱخْتَلَفُوا فِيهِ لَفِى شَكٍّ مِّنْهُ مَا لَهُم بِهِ مِنْ عِلْمٍ إِلَّا ٱتِّبَاعَ ٱلظَّنِّ وَمَا قَتَلُوهُ يَقِينًۢا بَل رَّفَعَهُ ٱللَّهُ إِلَيْهِ وَكَانَ ٱللَّهُ عَزِيزًا حَكِيمًا

"And [for] their saying, "Indeed, we have killed the Messiah, Jesus, the son of Mary, the messenger of Allah." And they did not kill him, nor did they crucify him; but [another] was made to resemble him to them. And indeed, those who differ over it are in doubt about it. They have no knowledge of it except the following of assumption. And they did not kill him, for certain. Rather, Allah raised him to Himself. And ever is Allah Exalted in Might and Wise." [77]

'Isa *'alayhis salaam* will remain in Heaven till his Second Coming towards the end of time. The Prophet *sallAllahu 'alayhi wa sallam* said,

"The Hour will not be established until the son of Mary [78] *descends amongst you as a just ruler..."* [79]

---

76   *Injeel* is the Arabic term for the Gospel of 'Isa *'alayhis salaam*.
77   Surah An-Nisaa' [4:157-158]
78   'Isa *'alayhis salaam*
79   Sahih Al-Bukhari

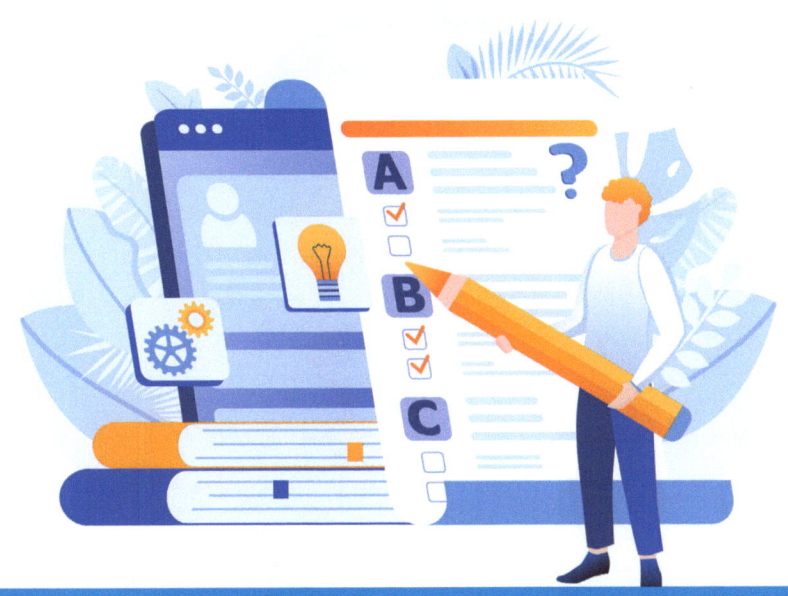

UNIT 2 CHAPTERS 4-5

REVIEW AND REFLECT QUESTIONS

1

Research and develop a diagram or infographic detailing the differences between Jewish, Christian, and Muslim beliefs in the Hereafter.

2

Is Christianity considered a monotheistic religion? Why or why not?

3

Make a comparison chart showing the differences in belief on 'Isa *alayhis salaam* in Christianity and Islam.

4

Create an infographic showing the similarities between Judaism and Islam.

5

Who are considered *"People of the Book,"* and why were they given that title in the *Qur'an*?

CHAPTER 6

HINDUISM & BUDDHISM

Hinduism, one of the world's oldest religions, traces its origins to the ancient Indus Valley civilization in present-day India, dating back over 4,000 years. Its roots are intertwined with the religious and cultural developments of the Indian subcontinent. Unlike the monotheistic religions, Hinduism does not have a single founder or a unified system of beliefs; rather, it is characterized by diversity and flexibility.

The sacred texts of Hinduism, known as the *Vedas*, form the foundation of the religion. These scriptures contain hymns, rituals, and philosophical teachings that provide insights into early Hindu thought. Over time, Hinduism evolved, incorporating a vast array of beliefs, practices, and deities. The development of epics like the *Mahabharata* and the *Ramayana*, which contain moral and religious narratives, played a pivotal role in shaping Hindu thought.

Hinduism also gave rise to concepts such as **karma** (the law of cause and effect), **dharma** (one's duty or moral responsibility), and **moksha** (liberation from the cycle of birth and death). It is important to note that Hinduism is not a monolithic faith but encompasses a wide spectrum of beliefs and practices, with adherents worshiping a diverse pantheon of gods and goddesses. [80]

---

[80] The Comprehensive Encyclopedia of Religions, Sects, and Contemporary Parties - Hinduism.

HINDU BELIEFS

Hinduism is well known for its polytheistic beliefs, featuring a multitude of gods and goddesses, each symbolizing different aspects of the divine. Among the prominent deities are *Brahma*, who is the creator; *Vishnu*, the preserver; and *Shiva*, the destroyer. Devotees make choices about which deities to worship based on their individual inclinations and requirements. This belief system represents a stark contrast to Islam, where the oneness of Allah is upheld. In addressing the notion of multiple gods, Allah tells us,

لَوْ كَانَ فِيهِمَآ ءَالِهَةٌ إِلَّا ٱللَّهُ لَفَسَدَتَا فَسُبْحَٰنَ ٱللَّهِ رَبِّ ٱلْعَرْشِ عَمَّا يَصِفُونَ

"Had there been within them [i.e., the heavens and earth] gods besides Allah, they both would have been ruined. So exalted is Allah, Lord of the Throne, above what they describe." [81]

In Hinduism, there's a fundamental belief in reincarnation [82] and *karma,* [83] concepts that shape the cycle of life, death, and rebirth. Reincarnation means that when a person dies, their soul is reborn in a new body. This cycle is influenced by karma, which is the sum of a person's actions in past lives. Good deeds lead to a better future life, while negative actions result in a less fortunate one. The ultimate aim is to break free from this cycle and attain liberation from earthly existence. Unlike the concept of heaven and hell, Hindus believe in a continual process of reincarnation until one reaches a profound spiritual level of unity with the divine or attains enlightenment. Hinduism promotes various beliefs and practices. Rituals, prayers, offerings, and meditation are just some of the practices of Hinduism. All of these are aimed at attaining a better spiritual connection with the divine.

---

81 Surah Al-Anbiyaa' [21:22]

82 Reincarnation: belief that a soul is reborn after death as another person, animal, or divine being.

83 ***Karma:*** The belief that somebody's good and bad actions in one of their lives will decide what will happen to them in their next life.

ISLAMIC VIEWPOINT

As Muslims, we hold a different perspective on the concepts of reincarnation and *karma*. Our belief centers on submission to Allah and the fulfillment of our religious duties. We firmly believe in the Day of Judgment, where every individual will be held accountable for their deeds in this life, standing before Allah. Depending on these actions, individuals will either be rewarded with entry into heaven or face punishment in hell in the hereafter.

DID YOU KNOW?

It is not permissible for Muslims to do Yoga. Yoga is a form of worship that comes from Hinduism; it involves various exercises and rituals, but the most problematic of them is an exercise called Surya Namaskar, known as the *"Sun Salutation,"* which is a yoga pose that prostrates to the sun on eight parts of the body. These parts are the two feet, the two knees, the two hands, the chest, and the forehead. For this reason, it is not permissible for Muslims to practice Yoga. Even if you only practice it for physical fitness, its roots are firmly entrenched in polytheistic beliefs, which contradict Islamic monotheism.

BUDDHISM

Buddhism, established around 2,500 years ago in ancient India by Siddhartha Gautama, widely known as the Buddha, has a compelling origin story. The Buddha's own life journey was characterized by his pursuit of enlightenment and his eventual discovery of the Four Noble Truths, which became the foundational teachings of Buddhism. These truths revolve around the understanding of suffering, its causes, and the path to achieving liberation from suffering.

After the Buddha's death, his followers passed on his teachings through spoken word and written scriptures. As Buddhism spread, it evolved into various schools, adapting to the diverse cultures it encountered across Asia. This diversity gave rise to distinct Buddhist traditions and practices.

The expansion of Buddhism across regions such as Southeast Asia, East Asia, and the Himalayas was made possible by trade networks and cultural exchanges. Additionally, the development of Buddhist art, architecture, and literature played a crucial role in popularizing the religion. Today, Buddhism remains a global philosophy with millions of adherents who embrace its core values of compassion, mindfulness, and the pursuit of spiritual enlightenment. [84]

BUDDHIST BELIEFS

Buddhism, often seen as more of a philosophy than a conventional religion because it lacks a belief in a god figure, centers its teachings around the Four Noble Truths. These truths explore the essence of suffering, its origins, the means to alleviate it, and the path leading to its cessation. However, over time, the veneration of Buddha and the erection of statues in his honor have led to his worship and polytheism.

In addition to their core principles, Buddhists share beliefs in concepts like reincarnation and karma, similar to those in Hinduism. They maintain that life's ultimate purpose is to transcend the cycle of reincarnation through attaining enlightenment, which offers liberation from suffering.

The beliefs and philosophy of Buddhism are contrary to Islam and go against the core tenets of being a Muslim. It's important to note that Buddhism's beliefs and philosophy diverge from Islam's core beliefs. We believe the existence of suffering is a test of this worldly life, due to the effect of people's deeds and what they do. Islam considers it a test from Allah. Allah says,

وَلَنَبْلُوَنَّكُم بِشَىْءٍ مِّنَ ٱلْخَوْفِ وَٱلْجُوعِ وَنَقْصٍ مِّنَ ٱلْأَمْوَٰلِ وَٱلْأَنفُسِ وَٱلثَّمَرَٰتِ وَبَشِّرِ ٱلصَّٰبِرِينَ

"And We will surely test you with something of fear and hunger and a loss of wealth and lives and fruits, but give good tidings to the patient." [85]

And in another *ayah* Allah tells us,

وَمَآ أَصَٰبَكُم مِّن مُّصِيبَةٍ فَبِمَا كَسَبَتْ أَيْدِيكُمْ وَيَعْفُوا عَن كَثِيرٍ

"And whatever strikes you of disaster - it is for what your hands have earned; but He pardons much." [86]

---

84 The Comprehensive Encyclopedia of Religions, Sects, and Contemporary Parties - Buddhism.
85 Surah Al-Baqarah [2:155]
86 Surah Ash-Shuraa [42:30]

ISLAMIC VIEWPOINT

As Muslims, our faith is rooted in the belief that Allah has provided us with clear guidance and everything we need to fulfill our ultimate purpose, which is to worship Allah alone. Unlike Buddhism, where the search for purpose and enlightenment is central, Islam emphasizes the worship of the one true God, Allah.

In Islam, we find our purpose through submission to Allah's will, following His commandments, and living a life in accordance with the teachings of the *Qur'an* and the *Sunnah*. Our faith offers us a comprehensive manual for life, addressing matters of ethics, morality, spirituality, and social justice. We believe that Allah's divine guidance provides us with a path to attain spiritual fulfillment in this life and salvation in the hereafter.

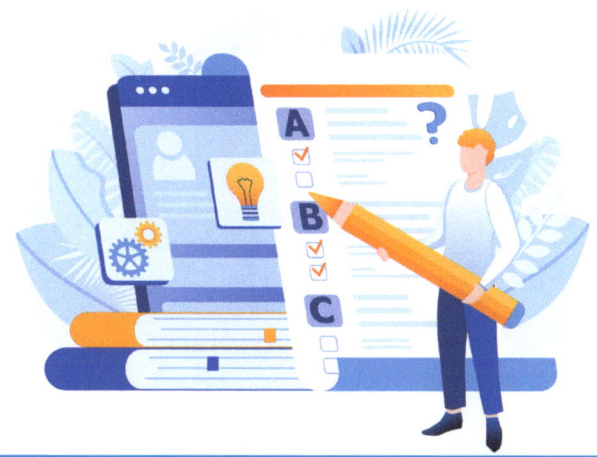

UNIT 2 CHAPTER 6

REVIEW AND REFLECT QUESTIONS

1

The word *"karma"* is often thrown around when someone has been wronged by someone else. Instead of getting back at a person, they trust that the universe will balance it out. Does the concept of *karma* exist in Islam? Would it be alright to use this term in our daily conversations? Why or why not?

2

Explain the Hindu and Buddhist concept of reincarnation. How does the concept of reincarnation go against the concept of the Day of Judgment as mentioned in the *Qur'an*?

3

Research and write two references from the *Qur'an* and *hadith* on the view of Idolatry in Islam.

4

Make a comparison chart of how Hinduism and Buddhism are similar and where they differ in their beliefs.

CHAPTER 7

DEISM, AGNOSTICISM, & ATHEISM

In the late 17th and 18th centuries, Europe found itself in the Enlightenment period, also referred to as the Age of Reason. It represents a time of scientific discovery and a strong emphasis on using reason and logic to understand the world around us. These views led to a departure from traditional religious beliefs and gave rise to new ideas and ideologies, including Deism, Agnosticism, and spreading Atheism.

DEISM

Deism rejects the belief in a God who directly interferes in human affairs or communicates through revelation. Instead, they believe in a Creator who established natural laws that governed the universe, allowing it to function independently. Deism initially gained popularity among intellectuals who sought to reconcile their rationalist views with their religious backgrounds. Deism became so popular that known historical figures like Thomas Paine, Voltaire, and Thomas Jefferson were Deists.

AGNOSTICISM

Agnosticism is an ideology that emerged as a result of the Enlightenment period. It is essentially a philosophical idea that aims to say, "We don't know" when it comes to God and the divine. Agnostics do not assert the existence or nonexistence of God but instead advocate for skepticism and an acknowledgment of the limitations of human reason and intellect. The term "agnosticism" was coined by the English biologist Thomas Henry Huxley, who advocated for the position that the ultimate nature of reality, particularly regarding the existence of God or gods, is fundamentally unknowable or beyond the scope of human knowledge. [87]

ATHEISM

Atheism is a philosophical stance that is characterized by the assumption that God does not exist. While atheistic ideas can be traced back to ancient civilizations, the explicit development of atheism as a distinct worldview gained prominence during the Enlightenment period. Philosophers like Denis Diderot and Baron d'Holbach, among others, contributed to the spread of atheistic thought. It is important to note that atheism encompasses a wide range of perspectives, from strong atheism, which asserts the nonexistence of God, to weak atheism, which simply lacks belief in God due to insufficient evidence (according to them). Atheists often prioritize empirical evidence, reason, and skepticism in forming their worldview and beliefs.

CONCLUSION

These ideologies that have emerged challenge the belief in God, ranging from complete denial of His existence, as held by atheists, to affirming the existence of a passive God, as believed by deists, while agnostics take a position somewhere between these two. Allah revealed Islam as guidance for all mankind, to inform humans about Himself and to correct and refute mere human opinions, misguided theories and conjecture about Him.

---

[87] The British Journal for the History of Science.

SUMMARY: WHAT IS DEISM? AGNOSTICISM? ATHEISM?

DEISM

1 God!

The belief in a single god who created the world but does not act to influence events. Deism is a philosophical system that acknowledges God but considers him a passive observer of his creation.

AGNOSTICISM

God???

A person who holds the view that any ultimate reality (such as God) is unknown and probably unknowable. One who is not committed to believing in either the existence or the nonexistence of God or a god.

ATHEISM

A person who disbelieves or lacks belief in the existence of God or gods.

Let us take a look at the following three points:

1. WERE THEY CREATED BY NOTHING?

ISLAMIC VIEWPOINT

As Muslims, we know that Allah exists, is ever-living, and is actively involved in maintaining the universe. The Qur'an provides a powerful argument for those who question His existence. Allah asks,

أَمْ خُلِقُوا مِنْ غَيْرِ شَيْءٍ أَمْ هُمُ ٱلْخَٰلِقُونَ
أَمْ خَلَقُوا ٱلسَّمَٰوَٰتِ وَٱلْأَرْضَ بَل لَّا يُوقِنُونَ

"Or were they created by nothing, or were they the creators [of themselves]?
Or did they create the heavens and the earth? Rather, they are not certain." [88]

From these *ayaat*, it becomes clear that Allah poses these questions as a way to show His existence.

This is a logical impossibility, because we all know that something cannot originate from nothing. Our own existence implies that we came from something and not nothing.

2. ARE THEY THEIR OWN CREATORS?

This is another impossibility, because something cannot create itself, leading to an infinite loop of self-creation.

3. DID THEY CREATE THE HEAVENS AND THE EARTH?

Did humanity create the universe, the planets, and all those things that are far greater than ourselves and surpass our ability. This is also another impossible position.

---

[88] Surah At-Toor [52:35-36]

For those who sincerely contemplate, it will be easy to see that God does exist. Allah tells us,

أَمْ لَهُمْ إِلَٰهٌ غَيْرُ ٱللَّهِ سُبْحَٰنَ ٱللَّهِ عَمَّا يُشْرِكُونَ

"Or do they have a god other than Allah? Glorified is Allah far above what they associate (with Him)!" [89]

The beliefs held by atheists, agnostics and deists are easily refuted by Allah in the *Qur'an*.

In conclusion, learning about the various sects among Muslims, major world religions, and ideologies helps us be more conscious of viewpoints and ideas that diverge from the Straight Path Allah wants us to follow. Learning about them is never to look down upon others but to help us steer clear from deviation. As Muslims, we need to be aware of these ideologies and how Islam provides guidance to lead people out of confusion and darkness toward the light of Allah.

As the Prophet *sallAllahu 'alayhi wa sallam* advised us, *"Leave what makes you doubt for what does not make you doubt. Verily, truth brings peace of mind and falsehood sows doubt."* [90]

Allah has already informed us that the right guidance is clear from what is falsehood

---

89 Surah At-Toor [52:43]
90 At-Tirmidhi

as He tells us,

قَد تَّبَيَّنَ ٱلرُّشْدُ مِنَ ٱلْغَيِّ ۚ فَمَن يَكْفُرْ بِٱلطَّـٰغُوتِ وَيُؤْمِنۢ بِٱللَّهِ فَقَدِ ٱسْتَمْسَكَ بِٱلْعُرْوَةِ ٱلْوُثْقَىٰ لَا ٱنفِصَامَ لَهَا ۗ وَٱللَّهُ سَمِيعٌ عَلِيمٌ

"...the truth stands out clearly from falsehood. So whoever renounces false gods and believes in Allah has certainly grasped the firmest, unfailing hand-hold. And Allah is All-Hearing, All-Knowing." [91]

Once Umm Salamah *radhiAllahu 'anha* [92] asked the Prophet *sallAllahu 'alayhi wa sallam*, "O Messenger of Allah, why do you supplicate so frequently, 'O Turner of the hearts, keep my heart firm upon Your religion?' He said, 'O Umm Salamah! Verily, there is no human being except that his heart is between Two Fingers of the Fingers of Allah, so whomsoever He wills, He makes steadfast, and whomever He wills, He causes to deviate.'" [93]

May Allah increase us in knowledge, grant us the humility to correct ourselves if we have strayed from His path, the courage to accept and follow the truth, and keep our hearts firm on the Straight Path that He has specified for us. Ameen.

---

91   Surah Al-Baqarah [2:256]

92   One of the wives of the Prophet *sallAllahu 'alayhi wa sallam*.

93   At-Tirmidhi

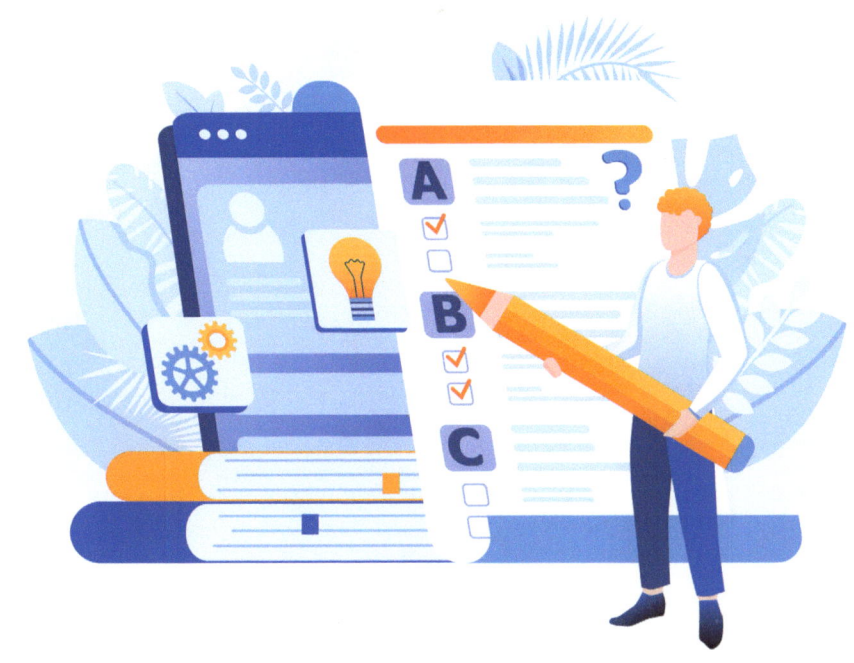

UNIT 2 CHAPTER 7
REVIEW AND REFLECT QUESTIONS

1

Identify Deism, Agnosticism, & Atheism in a social media influencer or famous person.

2

Research and write two *ayaat* that you can share with an Atheist to prove the existence of Allah.

3

There is a famous quote: *"There are no atheists on a sinking ship."* What do you think this means? Can you quote a verse from the *Qur'an* that supports this idea?

www.ingramcontent.com/pod-product-compliance
Lightning Source LLC
Chambersburg PA
CBHW042025150426
43198CB00002B/66